Including Children with Visual Impairment in Mainstream Schools

Including Children with Visual Impairment in Mainstream Schools

A Practical Guide

PAULINE DAVIS

David Fulton Publishers
London

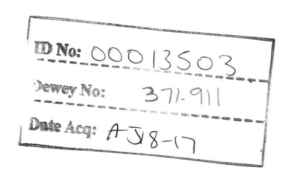

David Fulton Publishers Ltd
The Chiswick Centre, 414 Chiswick High Road, London W4 5TF

www.fultonpublishers.co.uk

David Fulton Publishers is a division of Granada Learning, part of the Granada Media Group.

First published 2003
10 9 8 7 6 5 4 3 2 1

British Library Cataloguing in Publication Data
A catalogue record for this book is available from the British Library.

ISBN 1 85346 914 9

Typeset by Textype Typesetters, Cambridge
Printed and bound in Great Britain by Ashford Colour Press Limited, Gosport, Hants

Contents

The author

Dr Pauline Davis is Lecturer in Education at the University of Manchester and Programme Director M.Ed. Special and Inclusive Education. She is a member of the Institute for Teaching and Learning. Recently, she directed research funded by the Economic and Social Research Council (ESRC R000223108), 'Including Visually Impaired Children in the Primary School Classroom', and is currently co-director of research in the inclusion of children with Down's syndrome, funded by the Nuffield Foundation. She has published in several journals including *JORSEN*, *Education 3–13* and *JET*. Pauline Davis has worked as an educational researcher on a number of funded research projects and has a particular interest in research methodology.

Acknowledgements

The project 'Including Visually Impaired Children in the Primary School Classroom' was fortunate in being able to employ a Research Associate, Dr Vicky Hopwood, who also had a major input into the research. While Vicky's career path has meant that she was unable to co-author this book, the findings of the inquiry are often presented in terms of 'we' in accord with the collaborative nature of the inquiry. Her contribution – in particular the content of the case studies – is fully acknowledged and her hard work and thoughtful comments greatly appreciated.

I would like to thank and acknowledge the input of everyone else who participated in the research; all the pupils, their parents and school and service staff who took part; those who gave up their time to be interviewed and those who permitted us to observe and discuss their working practices. By doing so they have helped in making this a publication that is grounded in the experiences of people's lives and in the realities of the contexts and circumstances of schools and their staff.

I would also particularly like to thank all those who commented and helped with the staff development session, especially students on the M.Ed Special and Inclusive Education course at the University of Manchester and service staff who participated in the research.

Many direct quotations from interviews are included in this book. I would like to acknowledge the hard work of Clare Davis and Lesley Brien, who painstakingly transcribed all the interviews.

The names of the schools, staff and children have been changed to maintain anonymity.

1 Introduction

Including children with visual impairment

Research studies have shown consistently the benefits of increasing access to opportunities for social interaction and learning for children with visual impairment (VI). Teaching children in mainstream schools carries inherent benefits of participation and learning within an environment of non-segregation, thus promoting the child's educational and social inclusion. However, children with VI also require additional support, e.g. in mobility or tactile awareness, in addition to accessing the main curriculum. Providing for children who are blind or who have low vision in the mainstream sector increases the diversity of needs in the classroom and presents challenges for schools to become more educationally inclusive.

How do teachers and other professionals manage to include effectively a child who is visually impaired in a classroom alongside, perhaps, 30 sighted peers? What is visual impairment and how might the educational needs of this group of children differ from those of children who are fully sighted? What is meant by the term inclusion and how has its meaning changed over the last few years? How can teachers, teaching assistants and other professionals learn to work together in ways that can increase the educational inclusion of the child? This book addresses these questions, and many others, and is intended to be of practical use to a wide range of practitioners who are concerned with developing more inclusive practices in primary schools and classrooms, especially with regard to the inclusion of children with VI.

Including Children with Visual Impairment in Mainstream Schools is aimed at teachers, special educational needs coordinators (SENCOs) head teachers in mainstream primary schools, and other professionals involved in the move to inclusive education, e.g. visiting teachers, teaching assistants, sensory service or visual impairment service managers or local education authority (LEA) officers. It should also be useful for parents of children with VI in increasing their awareness of the educational needs of their child. In addition, this book will be of relevance to students on PGCE, continuing education and Masters degree courses in Special or Inclusive Education. It supports primary schools and support services in their quest to develop more educationally inclusive practices – not only for children with VI, but for other children with more specific individual needs. The book is written to be a vehicle for whole-school professional development or for the professional development of the individual teacher. It provides:

- Staff development materials for use by the whole school, in small groups or by individuals.
- Case studies of schools committed to developing inclusive practices for children with VI.
- Evidence from new research that is grounded in the realities of teaching and learning in mainstream schools.

The catalyst for this book is the Economic and Social Research Council (ESRC) research project 'Including Children with Visual Impairment in the Mainstream Primary Classroom', which is based on case studies of 17 schools in the North-West of England. The first phase of the research involved observation of lessons and interviews with over 80 staff, including head teachers, class teachers, visiting teachers for the visually impaired, teaching assistants and support service managers. During the second phase of the study we worked closely with a small number of schools as they sought to develop more inclusive practices. Real examples from these schools – along with the dilemmas they faced and how these were overcome as the schools worked towards inclusion – provide the mainstay of the book.

In this first chapter, I define the use of the term 'visual impairment', introduce the reader to the research inquiry upon which this book is based, explain some of the reasons why the research was needed and provide details of the policy documentation and relevant legislation. The chapter ends with an outline of the content of the remaining chapters and staff development materials.

Visual impairment

The term 'visual impairment' refers to children who are classed as blind or as having low vision. There are various definitions, but the World Health Organisation (WHO) definitions of terms, based on visual acuity scores, are now the most widely accepted. These scores are based on the sight perception of people with 'perfect' vision and are written as a fraction. For example, a person with a score of 6/18 implies that he can see when 6 metres from an object what a person with perfect sight would see at 18 metres. Alternatively, a score of 3/60 means that an object at a distance of 3 metres appears in its detail as it would to a person with perfect sight if it were 60 metres away. According to this conception:

- a person scoring between 6/6 and 6/18 is classed as having normal vision;
- a person scoring between 6/18 and 3/60 is classed as having low vision;
- a person scoring less than 3/60 is classed as being blind.

Importantly, the vast majority of people who are classed as blind have some sight, i.e. usually, the term blind does not mean unable to see anything at all. Sometimes a person with no sight facility is referred to as being *totally blind*.

While this definition is useful in making a distinction between those with more severe and those with more moderate loss of sight – as might be required for purposes of resourcing or for other purposes of special entitlement – there are dangers associated with any forms of classification of people as the very act of placing someone in a group serves to mask diversity.

There are many different eye conditions and sight can be affected in many different ways. For example, a person classed as blind might have peripheral vision, another person might also be classed as blind but have tunnel vision, while yet another might find that his/her ability to see very much depends on the level of light available. For some people, too much light might lead to blindness, for others too little light may result in reduced vision. Some eye conditions might be more or less stable over time, others are degenerative. Near or distance vision might be affected. These are just a few examples – there are many more ways in which sight can vary.

The term *functional vision* serves a useful purpose. In contrast to the WHO definition, which is deficit in construction (i.e. focusing on what a person cannot see), functional vision refers in a positive way to available sight (i.e. focusing on what a person can see) and so opens possibilities of discussion of how sight can be used. The conception of functional vision also allows for a diversity of eye conditions and syndromes. In the context of school, a specialist teacher will acquire an in-depth understanding of a child's unique functional vision and how it might change over time. The specialist will work to optimise the sight available to the child by teaching him/her how to make best use of functional vision. This information will then be passed on to the class teacher and others who need to know it in order to help the child.

There are various other ways of classifying people with VI. Mason and

McCall (1997) use the generic term 'visual impairment' to describe a continuum of sight loss. They state that 'the term blind is used to describe children who rely predominantly on tactile methods in their learning e.g. Braille, while the term low vision is used with reference to children who are taught through methods which rely on sight' (Mason and McCall 1997: 2). This classification seems most appropriate in a context of education and is adopted where a distinction seems necessary.

Background to the research

There are an estimated 23,000 children with VI in the UK – including those with low vision and those who have additional disabilities – of which 9,000 are in primary school (Clunies-Ross and Franklin 1997). Fifty-three per cent of children with VI attended a local mainstream school in 1988 and this figure rose to 59 per cent in 1995 (Walker *et al*. 1992; Clunies-Ross and Franklin 1997). Although the proportion of children with VI in mainstream schools in the year 2002 is at the time of writing unknown, given the impetus for inclusive education, children with VI are likely to continue entering mainstream education in growing numbers. However, while normative findings such as this are useful in providing information on national trends, they can be misleading at a local level because of the great variability in the proportions of children in mainstream education (and the nature of that provision) between local education authorities (LEAs): in some authorities provision in the mainstream is now close to 100 per cent. However, interpretation of available statistics is not straightforward as simple percentages can mask realities, for instance by some parents choosing for their children to be educated in special provision in a neighbouring authority.

It is also useful to make a distinction between children with VI but no other additional difficulties and a larger group who have VI in combination with a range of additional difficulties (e.g. Walker *et al*. 1992 cited in Arter *et al*. 1999). Children with VI and additional difficulties are more likely (at the time of writing) to be educated in special schools or be attached to a resource unit (a special unit within a mainstream school) than children with no additional difficulties. Usually, the decision as to where a child will be educated is taken after a period of negotiation between the parents and education authority staff, e.g. the head of service for the visually impaired or sensory impaired. Parents have considerable rights in choosing the type of provision for their child. However, in many cases it is the *ability* of parents to exercise their rights that is instrumental in school selection, thus empowering those parents who are better informed, the most vocal and with the best communication skills.

The New Code of Practice on Special Educational Needs (DfES 2001) has a clear expectation that pupils with special educational needs (SEN) will be included in mainstream schools. The government believes that when parents want a mainstream place for their child the education service should do everything possible to try to provide it. This applies to children with VI with no additional difficulty as well as children with VI with additional difficulties. Certainly, there is no reason (unless parents insist) why a child with VI and no additional difficulties should not be in the mainstream classroom, even if s/he is totally blind. Furthermore, many children with VI and additional difficulties are also very well catered for in mainstream schools.

West and Sammons (1996) have examined some of the particular strategies and adaptations made in schools in order to meet special educational needs. However, their research does not specifically address visual impairment (blind and low vision). Recent research gives guidelines for the provision of children with special needs in mainstream schools. For example, Mittler (1996) and Venables (1998) link good practice with staff development, and Mortimer (1996) provides strategies for facilitating the teaching of young children. Sebba and Sachdev (1997) offer a thorough review of inclusive policies and address issues that impact on inclusive education including legislation, school organisation and classroom practice. These authors, however, do not focus on the particulars of practice relating to teaching children with VI in mainstream primary schools.

Guidelines have been written for practitioners concerning: services for visually impaired children (Hegarty *et al.* 1981; Dawkins 1991), and many authorities have up-to-date in-house information for schools available); teaching approaches (Best 1992) and practical advice for the mainstream teacher (Arter *et al.* 1999; Chapman and Stone 1998; Mason and McCall 1997; Torres and Corn 1990). Factors that impact on the quality of education that a child with VI receives include the physical environment of the school, social and cognitive factors, for example, whether or not the built environment is easy to navigate and free from obstacles, or whether the child's lighting needs are met in the context of a busy classroom.

Research in the field of educational inclusion has tended to focus on all the children in a classroom or in a school, rather than on a particular group of children. In this respect our approach was somewhat unusual as, in the schools we visited, we focused on a particular child, rather than on all the children in the class. It is through studying the inclusion of particular groups of children that

5

the gap between policy rhetoric and practice reality can be lessened, as cognitively it becomes easier to understand the complexities of the special need under examination, while still maintaining a mainstream focus. This is especially true for children classed as having low incidence special educational needs such as VI. As McCall (1999) has argued, because of their low frequency, disabilities such as VI have a tendency to be overlooked in grand designs.

There are a number of important reasons why the education of children with VI requires particular attention. First, visual impairment is an umbrella term for a wide variety of conditions, with the detailed practicalities for inclusion depending very much on the particular condition of a child. Specialist diagnosis and expert advice are essential to ensure that the specific visual needs of a child can be met. Secondly, children with VI often have complex needs which call for accommodation by the class teacher to ensure that they are afforded their full entitlement to the curriculum (Arter *et al.* 1999). For example, children with VI can quickly become visually fatigued when concentrating on school work for sustained periods of time and so may require regular periods of rest for their eyes. Current research also indicates that reading through Braille imposes significant cognitive demands for blind children compared with their sighted peers who read through print (Greaney *et al.* 1999). Thirdly, children with severe VI are likely to require additional support in developing social and life skills. For instance, Webster and Roe (1998) have highlighted the importance of social encounters to promote visually impaired children's cognitive, linguistic and social development. In addition, because policies and practices for educating children with VI are known to vary widely across LEAs, and because VI is a low incidence need, there are particular implications regarding the professional development of mainstream class teachers and teaching assistants.

In Britain, children classed as visually impaired who are in mainstream education should receive support from an outside service (part of the LEA) that is responsible for meeting the specific needs of the children. The visiting teacher (often, but not always, a qualified teacher of the visually impaired) is employed by the service and is usually responsible for supporting a caseload of children who are based in a number of schools. The visiting teacher often works in an advisory capacity and, in the case of children with a severe VI, is a main provider of an additional curriculum that is devised to facilitate the child's access to the main curriculum and to promote social inclusion among peers. This includes specialist teaching of Braille, mobility skills, tactile skills, keyboard skills and life skills. In addition to the time spent with a visiting teacher, the child with VI is likely to have a teaching assistant; for children who are classed as being blind, this support is likely to be full time. Teaching assistants usually provide support within the main classroom, whereas visiting teachers, because of their qualifications, have more flexibility in their work and may choose to withdraw the child for some periods from the main classroom – perhaps to a quiet area or to a special unit or designated room.

The teacher should expect to receive advice and guidance from the support service on how best to use the pupil's functional vision. This could mean removing reflective surfaces in the classroom, or for children with low vision providing clear, large print handouts. In most cases, teachers are encouraged to provide increased access to the curriculum via non-visual means such as through sound and touch. Teachers can expect to be provided with detailed information about the child's visual condition and ensuing educational implications. The support service responsible for VI should offer detailed guidance on appropriate teaching strategies, and use and adaptation of equipment and resources. We found that in most cases written guidance about the needs of an individual child was provided.

In order to ensure that the educational and sight needs of a child are met, it is crucial that guidance to teachers is of the highest standard. This requires the translation of a full medical diagnosis into guidance on the educational needs of a child. For example, a child may need to have his/her desk raised and perhaps at an angle of 20 per cent; alternatively, for some children, enlarging a worksheet is ineffective in helping them to see better. Mainstream teachers and support staff need to receive accurate and ongoing advice. Since there is a spectrum of conditions associated with VI, and the nature of a particular child's condition and needs is likely to change over time, providing this type of advice to the school and class teacher is crucial. Many would argue it is a role that requires a qualified teacher of the visually impaired (QTVI). Similarly, teaching a child Braille requires the expertise of a QTVI and a trained mobility officer must provide the mobility training. The need for expertise is also reflected by Farrell *et al.* (1999), who state that 'for [teaching assistants] who are likely to work with a specified group of pupils with identified disabilities, e.g. pupils with visual disabilities, some proven expertise in this area may be a necessary condition of the appointment. If it is not, then appropriate training should be provided immediately the post has been filled.'

About the research

Very little research has examined empirically the ways that children with VI are currently provided for in mainstream primary classrooms. Our inquiry has gone some way in addressing this gap and has examined teaching practices in mainstream primary school classrooms. The research agenda was addressed by the following questions:

- What are the circumstances of teaching and learning in mainstream primary schools with respect to children with VI?
- What can we find out about teaching practices, e.g. to do with method, use of support teachers or teacher development, that can facilitate a greater inclusion of children with VI?
- How can such practices be encouraged within schools?

The research inquiry comprised case studies of 17 mainstream primary schools selected in conjunction with the services responsible for VI in six LEAs in the North-West of England. In each school, interviews were conducted with all staff who had a stake in the education of the child with VI in the school. Where possible, interviews were conducted with the head teacher, the special educational needs coordinator (SENCO), the visiting teacher (peripatetic teacher), the teaching assistant (TA) and the class teacher. In addition, when we could we talked with the children and their parents.

LEAs were selected to reflect a variety of policies for the provision of children who are visually impaired. Participating LEAs included: Bury, Cheshire, East Lancashire, Manchester, Oldham and Trafford. Access to the schools was made in conjunction with the service responsible for VI in each LEA. Schools were selected to provide interesting and contrasting practices, contexts and needs to study (Taylor and Bogdan 1984). In particular, they were chosen as providing access to children with a wide range of visual impairments, ages and abilities.

Twenty-three children participated in this study: 12 boys and 11 girls. The children ranged in age from 4 to 12 years of age. Five of the children were Braille users and three of the children had documented additional difficulties. Most of the children we visited attended their local mainstream primary school, which was the choice of the child's parents made in consultation with the service and school. There were 13 mainstream schools without an additional attached unit or resource base for the visually impaired. One school housed the area resource base for children with VI, one school was resourced specifically for pupils with VI and two schools were resourced for children with special educational needs, for example, one had a unit for children with moderate learning difficulties (MLD).

All 23 children were observed in a learning situation on at least six occasions: two with the teacher, two with the teaching assistant and two with the visiting teacher. All children were observed in Literacy or Numeracy Hour sessions and a less prescribed lesson. Six children were selected for further observation sessions on the basis that the teaching offered something particularly interesting or because the specific needs of the child posed various challenges for his/her effective inclusion in the learning process. A videotape was made of the six children during a lesson in the main classroom. The observation sessions were followed, where possible, by informal discussions with the teachers, which concentrated on their understandings and interpretations of the classroom situation (Denzin and Lincoln 1998).

Outline of the book

The remainder of this book can be usefully divided into three sections. Chapter 2 discusses the contexts and circumstances of the teaching and learning in mainstream schools for children with VI. This is followed by case studies of four schools (Chapters 3 to 6) offering a variety of responses to inclusion and operating in very different circumstances. The third section of the book (Chapters 7 to 9) focuses on the development of educational inclusion for children with VI in the classroom. This section should enable teachers and others to acquire the knowledge required to teach a child with VI in a mainstream context.

Many of the chapters contain professional development sessions. In Chapters 2 and 9 these are intended for use for whole-school development; in Chapters 3, 6 and 7 they are for use by small teams of staff, and are written particularly with the class teacher, teaching assistant and visiting teacher in mind. The session in Chapter 8 can be used independently and is likely to be of most value to teaching assistants and teachers.

I previously believed that a blind child needs such specific help that there was no place for them in an ordinary school but I have been proved wrong . . . [Joanne] is the advert of inclusion.

[class teacher]

At first when she came to school, I must admit that I thought this is ridiculous. She came in with her walking frame and she couldn't see and she was slightly deaf in one ear and I felt there was no way this was going to work. And there's a special school that could support her, but she's done marvellously. I can see the advantage now . . . it isn't a problem at all. I agree with inclusion now. Seeing all the other children with her, that is definitely an advantage.

[class teacher]

The only way I could do it was for somebody to come in here and tell me . . . to give me advice about what to do and how to go about it . . . I wanted backup . . . [somebody] to say 'yes that's fine'.

[class teacher]

Chapter 2 explores the circumstances of teaching and learning in mainstream primary schools with respect to children with VI, and considers the roles of support teachers and staff development in the facilitation of educational inclusion for such children. It begins with an explanation of the term 'inclusion' and goes on to provide a framework for developing educational inclusion in schools; while the focus is on increasing the inclusion of children with VI, the framework should also serve as a basis for developing the quality of inclusion for other children in the school. Related issues concerned with communication between staff, working with others in the classroom and staff development are discussed. Chapter 2 also serves to illustrate the wide variety of views held by teachers and others concerning the inclusion of children with VI in mainstream schools. All the suggestions for the good practice of teaching children with VI were observed at least once in the field, unless otherwise stated.

2 Towards an understanding of inclusion

The social development of the child is an essential part of the ongoing development of his/her participation and learning in school. Learning presupposes a specific social nature and a process by which children grow into the intellectual life of those around them. Indeed, a belief in socially constructed knowledge makes it difficult to separate the idea of children's social inclusion in the learning process from their development. Webster and Roe (1998) have highlighted the importance of social encounters to promote visually impaired children's cognitive and linguistic as well as social development. Like many others, we point to the need for developing teaching practices that:

- Lead to greater social inclusion in the learning activities taking place in the classroom.
- Lead to increased access to the curriculum.
- Develop the child's independence.
- Provide equality of opportunity.

It might now be helpful to point out a distinction between the term *inclusion*, which is frequently and currently used with regard to teaching children with special educational needs in mainstream schools, and the term *integration*, which was also (and sometimes still is) used to mean teaching children with special educational needs in mainstream schools. While these terms might appear to be similar, or even synonymous, there are important distinctions that should be made.

The term 'integration' can be associated with the medical model of disability in which problems in education are considered as residing with the individual. Hence, that individual must adapt, fit or integrate with the existing system of the school. 'Inclusion' goes hand-in-glove with the social model of disability. The social model implies that disabilities are as much products of the environment, attitudes and institutional practices as the impairment itself. By altering attitudes and institutional practices, schools can do much to reduce barriers to access and participation. Inclusion, therefore, involves a different

11

approach, whereby attempts are made to resolve difficulties within the school, rather than accepting difficulties within the child. The difference between *integration* and *inclusion* is highlighted in the case studies in Chapters 3–6.

It has been argued that developing a language for inclusion is important as ascribing educational problems to pupil deficits may conceal barriers to learning and participation, and hinder opportunities for the development of school policies and practices for all (Booth *et al.* 2000: 13; Ainscow *et al.* 1999). Moreover, as others have argued, inclusion 'requires a detailed and precise definition, for otherwise there is a danger that schools can claim that their provision is inclusive when the opposite may well be the case' (Feiler and Gibson 1999).

Defining inclusion

One important theme emerging from our data was that there is no one consistent meaning afforded to the term 'inclusion' and so we concur with the views outlined earlier. Examples of definitions used by teachers during our inquiry were:

- *Enabling access to the curriculum to the same level as the others by adapting resources or teaching methods for him to do that, take part as fully as possible...*
- *To some extent it depends just what inclusion is ... inclusion, I think probably within the special school context it is about making sure that they can make the best of the curriculum that the school is offering, which I suppose is exactly what is happening in the mainstream too.*
- *Inclusion should be preparing for lifelong learning. If inclusion is only just in the school environment ... then it is not going to work ... We have to change the culture within schools and we have to change society.*

For many teachers, the term 'inclusion' is used synonymously with 'integration', the implication being that once the child is in the school then inclusion has taken place. To some inclusion meant good practice; for others, inclusion referred to inclusion in the community as a whole, not just in the school.

Thus, we came across:

- Inclusion as social inclusion.
- Inclusion as integration.
- Inclusion as something more than integration.
- Inclusion meaning 'fully participating in'.

- Inclusion meaning 'not withdrawal'.
- Inclusion meaning 'limited withdrawal from the main classroom'.
- Inclusive education meaning 'the development of unitary provision for all children'.
- Inclusive education meaning 'being taught in a mainstream setting some of the time'.
- Inclusive practice used to mean effective practice or good teaching or simply what is best for the child.

We consider inclusion as a means of increasing the child's participation socially and educationally in the classroom, the school and more generally in society. We therefore view the inclusion of the child in school not only in terms of his/her participation in the lesson but also in terms of his/her opportunity to participate and in terms of opportunities for developing the skills needed to live independently. Achieving *inclusion* will be described in relation to accessing the environment or buildings and decor of the school, participation in the lesson and social inclusion, and access to an additional curriculum required to enable independence.

SOCIAL AND	_____	Environmental access – school and class-room
EDUCATIONAL	_____	Inclusion/participation in the classroom, learning and social development
INCLUSION	_____	Additional curriculum specialist and support teaching

Environmental access

Buildings can be a problem ... And knowledge ... People are frightened of blindness and visual impairment.

[head of service]

Modifications to the school environment can help to secure equality of access for children with VI and facilitate a more independent way of living. Improving access to the physical environment of the school often can be achieved by:

- Using different floor coverings to enable a child with VI to navigate the school.
- Replacing swing doors and solid doors with see-through doors to reduce accidents.

- Installing window blinds to reduce glare.

The child can be assisted in navigating the building by using strategically placed Braille, tactile or large print signs.

Equality of access to the school playground, hallways and assembly halls can be improved by the use of white lining to mark out areas and highlight tips of stairs. Handrails may also be required.

> *We have plundered the access fund [and] put in carpet with different patterns, so [children with VI] can feel it, trails so the children can find their way to cloakrooms. We've put in ramps for the wheelchair users, and changed all the doors so you could see through the bottom half, people couldn't understand why you need to do that. But if you have a blind child who needs to find his way by touch, and you've got doors that open both ways, just as he is coming up to a door to feel if it's there, another child comes through the door in the other direction and knocks him down, because you can't see. So we've had all the panes taken out and plastic ones put in.*
>
> [head teacher]

Examples of good practice in playground design are incorporating both quiet and 'rowdy' play areas, and shaded areas suitable for children with photophobia (light sensitivity), purchasing plants which provide sensory stimulation for blind children and ensuring playground games such as hopscotch are clearly painted.

Wall displays can be made accessible by including tactile diagrams and positioning materials at an appropriate height. Examples of good practice include positioning work of the child who is blind at a height where the child can touch it, and producing displays in large font typefaces and at eye level for children with low vision.

The classroom environment

Children with VI often require the use of bulky equipment to enable them to take part more fully in the learning process. For example, they may need some of the following: electronic Braillers, computers, closed circuit televisions (CCTVs) and task lighting. These all require a power source and careful positioning so that there are no hazardous trailing cables. Unless modifications are made to the classroom, the position of power sources can prove a serious limitation as to where the child is seated, which may result in the child being separated from his/her peer group. The same can be true of reading stands and sloping desks as the child may be seated alone at a table, at the reading stand may limit interaction with the pupils opposite.

There are a number of examples of good practice that help to tackle this issue. The quickest and most cost-effective way is to move furniture and reorganise the classroom. Alternative strategies include offering the child a number of workstations, a position near the front of the class for board work, a position with peers for class work and an area close to another peer group for using CCTV. The child can be encouraged to be responsible for his/her own learning and to move to the appropriate position for the appropriate activity. In another instance, a school had purchased a trolley complete with power sockets for the CCTV. This not only frees up valuable space in the classroom, but also the CCTV can be easily transferred when required by the child or for classroom demonstration purposes.

For many children with VI, changing the physical environment is disorienting, so the teacher is advised to minimise rearrangements to class seating. This is contrary to advice on effective teaching that encourages teachers to be creative in their use of space.

Although the new *Special Educational Needs Code of Practice* (DfES 2001) views special educational needs as generic and therefore does not provide guidance for specific SEN, it might be worth pointing out that this was not the case with the draft code. The *Draft Special Educational Needs Code of Practice* (DfEE 2000) provided some useful guidance regarding teaching children with VI and stated that:

> for some children [with VI] the inability to take part fully in school life causes significant emotional stress or physical fatigue. Many of these children and young people will require some of the following:

> Flexible teaching arrangements
> Appropriate seating, acoustic conditioning and lighting
> Adaptations to the physical environment
> Adaptations to school policies and procedures
> Access to alternative or augmented forms of communication
> Provision of tactile or kineasthetic materials
> Access to low vision aids
> Access in all areas of the curriculum through specialist aids, equipment or furniture
> Regular and frequent access to specialist support

> (DfEE 2000: 65)

Inclusion/participation in the school and classroom

Opportunity for inclusion in all social events and school activities

She takes part in all activities, pantomimes, whatever we do, Mary is there. She is in the school choir. Umm, I can remember the music teacher . . . saying, how am I going to cope with this? And I said, you'll find it easy. The main thing was for Mary to know when to start and when to stop singing because she can't see the conductor. But soon it was sorted out and a child just stands next to her and squeezes her hand and that was it, that was her off! She is quite active as part of it.

[head teacher]

Providing opportunities for children with VI to participate fully in the life of the school is particularly important given that living with VI can often act as a hindrance to social development. Every attempt should be made to ensure that the child is afforded the chance to participate in school trips, PE, the playground and after-school activities.

Examples of good practice include offering support for pupils to go on school trips and providing transport so they can attend after-school activities. Further models of good practice are presenting sighted children with opportunities to learn skills and games usually only offered to children with VI, such as playing goal ball (a game for visually impaired and fully sighted children) and learning Braille. Inviting a guest speaker into the school to talk to the whole class/school about different types of VI can also facilitate social inclusion.

Participation in class

Enabling access to the curriculum to the same level as the others by adapting resources or teaching methods for him to do that, take part as fully as possible . . .

[class teacher]

I'd try not to place too much emphasis on things that I've written down, when we are talking and I suppose I always make sure things are repeated quite often . . . When he puts his hand up then I always ask him as soon as I . . . can because that is one of the things we are trying to encourage him to do . . . I suppose it's not a particularly natural thing for a blind person to do to . . . attract attention. I try and avoid being too visual . . . although you've got to cater for everybody not just him . . . I try if I'm using something visual to try and find some equivalent . . . [And I] make sure I repeat . . . anything that's written on the board.

[class teacher]

She is never excluded from any lesson, you adapt, even if it's art . . . You go to great lengths so as not to exclude children from the lesson . . . She trampolines when we go trampolining, she does everything really.

[class teacher]

In the case of children with some functional vision, the teacher is usually given advice and guidance from the support service on how best to use the pupil's available sight. In most cases, the teacher will be encouraged to provide increased access to the curriculum via non-visual means such as the hearing and touch senses. The teacher can expect to be provided with detailed information about the child's visual condition. The support service responsible for VI should offer detailed guidance on appropriate teaching strategies, and use and adaptation of equipment and resources. We found that in most cases written guidance about the needs of an individual child was provided.

Inclusion in the main activities taking place in the classroom is crucial for improving access to the curriculum and developing the child's social interaction skills and independence. The research showed that inclusion in the lesson can be facilitated by:

- Curriculum delivery via non-visual means in addition to a visually based presentation.
- Frequent use of participatory teaching methods.
- Clearly adapted teaching materials that the child with VI can understand (usually intended for use with whole class).
- The child with VI being positioned within the class so as to facilitate their interaction with others.
- The teaching assistant working in ways to enable the development of the child's independence; for instance, by also working with other children perhaps in a small group with the child who is visually impaired.

For example, during one of our visits to a school we observed a class working in groups on different activities. Most of the pupils were working independently while the class teacher worked with one particular table on group reading. Present in the classroom was a boy, Nathaniel, who was blind. He was engaged in a written activity alongside the children on his table and made use of an electronic Brailler. There was much discussion among the children about the writing, including the sighted pupils telling the blind child certain jargon and slang expressions. This activity provided an important opportunity for peer interaction and social development which, on this occasion, was facilitated by the fact that the teaching assistant, knowing the child was capable, had left him to get on independently.

Suhail, a boy in Year 1 with low vision and supported in school by a teaching assistant, provides another example. During the Literacy Hour, Suhail was seated at a table next to the carpet where the rest of the class were sitting. The class teacher conducted the shared reading activity from the front. The class was reading a poem, which was placed on a flip chart by the side of the teacher. Suhail had his own enlarged copy of the text, which was placed on a work stand on his desk. The teaching assistant sat next to Suhail, but at the far side of the room, so as not to separate the child from his peer group. The class teacher used a pointer to highlight the words in the text as the class read together. The teaching assistant had an identical pointer which she used in the same way to highlight the words of the text on Suhail's own copy. The class teacher took full responsibility for Suhail and checked he was following and keeping up. During class discussion, the class teacher allowed plenty of time before seeking answers to questions. In this way Suhail, with the help of his teaching assistant, when needed, was able to access the lesson and to provide answers equally alongside his peers.

This can be considered inclusive practice because:

- Suhail is part of the main lesson.
- The teaching assistant provides supplementary but not the sole input.
- Other children might also benefit from 'extra' time to assimilate information.
- The class teacher and teaching assistant are working in partnership.

Of particular benefit was the way in which the class teacher allowed Suhail time to formulate responses to questions and to follow and access the text. This meant that the teaching assistant did not have to reinforce work at the same time as the class teacher was addressing the rest of the class.

The additional curriculum

We define the additional curriculum as the skills, knowledge and behaviour needed to facilitate the child's access to the main curriculum and to promote social inclusion among peers, and more widely in society, e.g. mobility, tactile awareness and life skills. This is usually provided by the visiting teacher, who may be (and this is the preferred case) a QTVI.

Throughout the investigation we encountered a commonly held belief among the participants that it was not appropriate to teach some skills such as mobility, life skills and the initial stages of learning to Braille in the main

18

classroom. These additional skills were predominantly taught in periods of withdrawal from the main classroom. For example, teaching a child to tie a shoelace in the mainstream classroom was believed to be incongruent and likely to cause the child embarrassment. Alternatively, most of the participants in the inquiry believed that, initially, basic mobility skills are best learnt in an uncrowded, safe environment other than the main classroom. In our view, this specialist teaching was essential, often personal and appropriate.

> *There are certain things with a visually impaired child that you need to withdraw for . . . Braille for example . . . If you are developing listening skills, you can't do that in a noisy classroom or even a classroom with normal work going on . . . But I don't like to withdraw a child.*

[service staff member]

Mobility training must, by law, be provided by a qualified mobility officer, and mobility forms an important part of the additional curriculum; however, it is possible for mainstream class teachers and others to provide opportunities that reinforce the children's mobility in the classroom. To facilitate this, the class teacher, teaching assistant and visiting teacher must have the opportunity to meet and plan for the child's development.

> *We have trained people who are mobility officers but you've got the issue inclusive learning is about people belonging to the community they are in. It is no good saying the inclusive environment is only the environment of the school because life is much more than the school . . . When they go out, when they are in the home, you don't want them to feel isolated. So I feel very strongly that one side of education is training, to cross the road, to go to the shop. Now actually getting a mobility officer to go into school and do that or in the home as well, well they are like gold dust. The other issue is parents, over-protecting.*

[head of service]

However, where staff were able to work effectively as a team, the reinforcement of skills that the child had learned with a visiting teacher was in evidence in the mainstream. Examples of inclusive practice included providing opportunities for the child to use the skills s/he was developing out of class, in the main classroom or more widely in the school. For example, sending the child with a message for another teacher elsewhere in the school, or sending him/her to collect the register could reinforce mobility and orientation skills. Indeed, where the child with VI was engaged in the main body of the lesson, then withdrawal for a few hours with a specialist teacher did not seem to lead to the segregation of that child.

We have had her pouring liquid, you know say within capacity lessons . . . And you can easily transfer that to a cup of tea as she gets older . . . These things are ongoing in the classroom but they don't take over from curricular needs.

[class teacher]

Partnership between the teaching assistant and the teacher

The extent to which the teacher needs to work with other people in providing for the child with VI is obviously dependent on the level of support provided and the nature and severity of the child's VI. However, for many of the children we observed, additional support was considerable. For children classed as blind, this frequently equated to a full-time teaching assistant and several hours a week with a visiting specialist teacher of the visually impaired.

While the role of the teaching assistant varied, in all cases, the teaching assistant was responsible for producing teaching materials. This might be photocopying and adapting a big book for use in the Literacy Hour, Brailling the class reader or producing tactile maps, tables or charts. Indeed, the need to provide alternative materials for the child with VI, for most teaching assistants, comprised a main element of their role. Teachers stated that they needed to plan their lessons well in advance and to communicate their intentions to the teaching assistant. However, time for communication was often limited and on many occasions planning was done more on an ad hoc basis.

Variation in the role of the teaching assistant seemed to revolve around the extent to which she worked exclusively the child with VI. In some cases, the teaching assistant sat next to that child most of the time, as if conducting a tutorial with the child that was separate from the main body of the lesson. This way of working has been considered a pitfall of in-class support as it distracts the child's attention from the mainstream class teacher and serves to create 'a lesson within a lesson' (Welding 1996: 116). Where teaching was in parallel for extended periods of time, or was the sole means of teaching, it seemed to be to the detriment of the social inclusion of the child in the class.

Some staff expressed concern that the presence of a teaching assistant could result in the child becoming overly dependent on him or her, especially if the assistant is in the classroom on a full-time basis.

The school's point of view . . . [is] probably more important, that there is the right human attitude . . . and the class teacher who is immediately responsible . . . the person who is going to work with the child on a daily basis is the pivotal person [but] clearly the management need to be positive.

[LEA officer]

This concern about over-dependence on the teaching assistant has been highlighted in previous research literature (e.g. Booth 1995; Welding 1996; Quah and Jones 1997; Lynas 1999).

The danger that you can get . . . is that the class teacher doesn't take ownership of the child, and because there is . . . support there, they feel they can delegate the teaching responsibility . . . and don't see the child as theirs.

[head of service]

While there will be times when it is appropriate for the teaching assistant to work with the child in ways to prevent him/her being part of the main activity taking place in classroom, care is needed to enable the child to participate in the main lesson as much as possible.

Some of the best practice we observed was when the teaching assistant, visiting teacher and class teacher worked together in a team, sharing knowledge and skills, and diversifying in their roles. For instance, when the visiting teacher shares expertise about a child, e.g. about the development of mobility skills, the teaching assistant or class teacher can continue with this work on other occasions. Alternatively, the teacher might sometimes want to teach the child with VI individually or in a small group. At such times the teaching assistant needs to support other children in the class. It seems that children who Braille feel more included when the teacher makes the effort to learn a little about Braille, although it is not expected that the class teacher should be skilled in Braille.

Communication between the teacher, teaching assistant and visiting teacher

A significant barrier to communication was the lack of opportunity for the class teacher to meet and plan with the teaching assistant and visiting teacher. Although in many of the schools effective communication was in evidence, this tended to be on an informal or 'goodwill' basis.

[Because] that means finding time when the class teacher can talk casually . . . and isn't engaged with the class, and indeed has the time and energy perhaps . . . and space . . . It can often be a case of . . . five minutes whenever you can.

[visiting teacher]

Given the numerous demands on teachers' time it might be that formal provision for staff development is needed if class teachers and teaching assistants are to benefit fully from the expertise of the visiting teacher. Although the government is beginning to recognise the time-consuming nature of the role of the SENCO (DfEE 2000), more needs to be done to allow other members of staff working with children with special educational needs time to talk and plan.

> *People have to address the implications of how adults share knowledge, there has to be time for them to do that.*

[class teacher]

We argue, based on our many conversations with teachers, that such a move would have the support of the majority of mainstream primary school teachers:

> *I think the actual chat with the support worker was the most informative.*

[class teacher]

> *Being able to go on a training course or something like that . . . talking to people who are qualified . . . who can give me some expert knowledge and it's knowledge that I can then use in the classroom.*

[class teacher]

In summary, we found from our inquiry that a number of factors facilitated the sharing of practice. These were when:

- The roles of each member of the team – the visiting teacher, the class teacher and the teaching assistant – were considered as skilled and varied.
- Formal time was designated for communication between the visiting teacher, class teacher and teaching assistant.
- The visiting teacher made it a priority to disseminate specialist knowledge to class teachers and teaching assistants.
- Quality staff development and training for teaching assistants was in place.
- The teaching assistant was viewed as belonging to both the school community and the community of the service, responsible for VI.
- Opportunities were available for teaching assistants to meet with and observe other teaching assistants.

Staff development

Staff development, usually supplied by the relevant service for the visual impaired, had taken place in all the participating schools. In many of the schools we visited, the quality of available staff development relating specifically to the teaching of children with visual impairment was high; however, there was an inconsistency in the quality and quantity of staff development provided. For example:

> *I've been on a lot of courses. I learned the Braille and I learned mobility skills . . . I went on a two-day course for classroom support assistants, that was very useful because they came from all over the country and you could swap ideas . . . you learn quite a lot from that. I went to see how examination papers were prepared . . . I went on . . . a literacy course . . . I'm going on one tomorrow on the Literacy and Numeracy Hour.*
>
> [teaching assistant]

Alternatively we also came across children who were blind and were learning through Braille with teaching assistants who had inadequate, or in one case no, knowledge of Braille. This is a matter for concern and in our view is not acceptable.

Moreover, because VI is a low incidence special educational need, many teachers will never have taught a child with VI. For others this might be a one-off experience or an experience that happens every few years. It would be impractical (if not impossible) for mainstream teaching assistants and teachers to acquire the same level of expertise in VI as a visiting teacher or a specialist teaching assistant. However, staff development is advisable, not only for the staff who are working closely with a child who is visually impaired, but also for the whole school staff. For instance, there are many opportunities within a mainstream classroom that allow mobility skills to be developed. The mainstream teacher with a child who is visually impaired in the class, therefore, requires knowledge specific to the needs of the child in his/her class, as well as support in developing a wider repertoire of more inclusive teaching methods.

We therefore point to the need for guidance for mainstream teaching staff and appropriate and specialised training for teaching assistants, which echoes the findings of other researchers in the field.

Building for inclusion

Much can be done to enable a child with VI to fully participate in the school and classroom. While there is an important and necessary role for specialist teachers skilled in supporting children with VI, there are many opportunities for the class teacher to take ownership of the learning and teaching of children with VI and enable them to become fully participating members of the class. The importance of this – and the degree of teaching ability required to make the integration of many children with SEN educationally inclusive – should not be underestimated. Often advice that appears simple and unproblematic to implement requires much higher levels of knowledge, sensitivity and skill than is immediately apparent.

> *Our biggest problem is training . . . there's a huge shortage of skilled people out there and when you advertise there's a lack of response which is worrying. Not as many teachers are going into support service work because the government agenda hitherto has been discouraging that sort of. . .*
>
> *[head of services for the visually impaired]*

> *We are having real problems recruiting people who are sufficiently skilled and qualified and that . . . has a knock-on effect for the inclusion agenda because whilst we may be willing and parents may wish, if we can't get the staff to service the needs of these children, support our schools, then we are sometimes forced to look elsewhere, against our wishes.*
>
> *[head of services for the visually impaired]*

Summary

This chapter has served to expand upon the findings of our research. Importantly, it provides a framework for developing inclusion practices for children with VI in mainstream schools, which is used in the following chapters. An overview of the meaning and mechanisms for achieving effective inclusion was outlined and illustrated with direct quotations from some of the participants in the project. Education in the mainstream sector for children with VI is viewed as effective and achievable.

> *How Julie is now, I would define it as inclusion. She is part of the class, she is not excluded from anything and . . . I am very much aware of what is needed for her, and you accommodate that when you can, without making a fuss.*
>
> [class teacher]

> *Catering for the individual child really as best you can, meeting their needs, exploring their potential and making the school a worthwhile place for them. And one where they felt happy, secure, safe. I think the ethos of the school plays a big part in this because we have a strong emphasis on . . . the individual, on other children accepting children no matter what . . . race, creed or colour they may be.*
>
> [class teacher]

Whole-school development session: Raising awareness

This session is intended to facilitate whole-school development on inclusion. It is for all members of the school community and is intended for use in a one-hour session. Members of staff who will be working closely with a visually impaired child will also require additional training.

It would be useful for a QTVI – who is familiar with the educational needs of the child with VI – to be present. Alternatively, the SENCO may prefer to discuss the educational needs of the child and his/her sight condition with the specialist teacher prior to this session.

This session focuses on the following themes:

- Expectations
- Staffing and support
- Specific information regarding the needs of the child
- Environmental access
- Social inclusion

Expectations

At first when she came to school, I must admit that I thought this is ridiculous. She came in with her walking frame and she couldn't see and she was slightly deaf in one ear and I felt there was no way this was going to work. And there's a special school that could support her, but she's done marvellously. I can see the advantage now . . . it isn't a problem at all. I agree with inclusion now. Seeing all the other children with her, that is definitely an advantage.

[class teacher]

Teachers and others often feel anxious when contemplating the inclusion of a child with VI, especially if the child is blind and they have no prior experience of the inclusion of a child with limited functional vision. Their concerns might be for the child's safety, about how the child will be able to learn in the environment of a busy class, about how other children will react and about how much time will be needed to make the required level of provision. In our experience such concerns are typical, and pass once the staff concerned can see how successfully a child who is severely visually impaired can be included as a fully participating member of the school community.

Task

Make a list of the concerns of all those present in this session. It may be helpful if each person were to voice the concern that they believe might be most relevant to their role in the educational inclusion of the child. For instance, if you are the dinner lady then you may be concerned about the child's ability to eat independently.

List of concerns

Staffing and support

What is the name of the child and in which year group will s/he be placed?

When is the child due to join the school?

Who would be the main members of staff working with the child from within the school?

Are additional staff involved from outside the school?

What are their names and roles?

How often will they be in school?

Which service or organisation are they from?

Who are the parents of the child?

Are they involved parents?

Are they visually impaired?

Specific information regarding the needs of the child

What is the nature of the child's VI?

Blind/low vision

Special medical terms, e.g. nystagmus

Does the child have additional difficulties?

If so, what is the nature of these?

The generic term visual impairment is used to describe the continuum of sight loss. Where a distinction is necessary, the term blind is used to describe children who rely predominantly on tactile methods in their learning, while the term low vision is used with reference to children who are taught through methods, which rely on sight

(Mason and McCall 1997: 2)

Educationally blind is defined as functional sight less than 3/60. At best the child can see at a distance of 3 metres what a typically sighted person would see at 60 metres.

- Low vision is regarded as between 3/60 and 6/60.
- Totally blind – when the child has no functional sight.

Task

Look out of the window – how well can you see an object 60 metres away? This is likely to be the sort of detail that the child will see when looking at the chalkboard. What are the suggested educational implications for your child?

Educational implications for

27

Environmental access

It may be that major adaptations to the school building will be required; alternatively, any adaptations will be minor. Most schools will arrange a visit from the service for the visually impaired. A qualified teacher of the visually impaired should accompany senior members of the team on a walkabout of the school premises in order to identify safety issues and necessary adaptations.

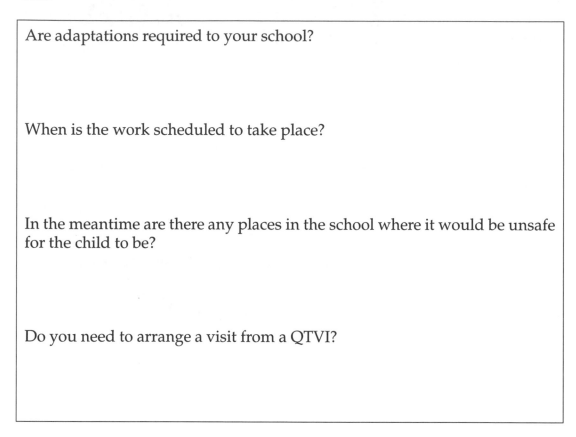

> Are adaptations required to your school?
>
>
> When is the work scheduled to take place?
>
>
> In the meantime are there any places in the school where it would be unsafe for the child to be?
>
>
> Do you need to arrange a visit from a QTVI?

Care should be taken by *all* staff regarding classroom and corridor displays, and clear signs should be in place throughout the school. Displays for children who are blind should be positioned at an appropriate height so the child can touch them. For children with low vision, use a large font size for displays and place them at eye level for accessibility. Many useful tips for displaying work can be found in Arter *et al.* (1999).

Braille or tactile labels were used in some schools together with clear print to signpost children with VI.

Displays
Decide on a whole-school strategy for displaying work.

Discuss how to achieve clear signing.

Buildings should be clearly marked as appropriate, e.g. using Braille signs, white-painted tipped stairs, etc.

Social inclusion

Children with VI should be given every opportunity to participate in school activities to the same degree as any other typically sighted child. For example, to take part in:

- pantomimes or other school plays
- assemblies
- sports events
- eating with his/her peers
- opportunity to play with his/her peers
- travelling to and from school

While safety is paramount and must always remain so, there is a danger that adults can be over-protective, e.g. in their use of language, body language and behaviour. On occasions this might be appropriate, but very often such behaviour is symbolic of attitudes that ultimately will not promote the developing independence of the child.

3 Case study: Pilkingston Primary School

Entering the classroom

It is the Literacy Hour and Year 5, as usual, is being taught by the Year 6 teacher who comes into the class to take the literacy session four times a week. The topic is 'Instructions' and the class is reading a recipe together. The classroom is of average size but the room is crowded as it contains 37 children. In an attempt to make sure that they can see the shared text, the teacher has grouped most of the children towards the front of the room, where she has placed a copy of the big book on a reading stand and a second copy on an overhead projector (OHP). The pupils read the recipe aloud and then discuss features of the text: the way it is formatted, how the pictures help to clarify instructions and the style in which it is written.

There are three members of staff present in the room – the teacher, the general teaching assistant and the teaching assistant assigned for Sanjeev, who is educationally blind. As the teacher talks, the general teaching assistant sits at a table with a group of children, some of whom are classified as having special educational needs. On the next table sits Joseph, a child with moderate learning difficulties (MLD) and low vision. To the right of the room, sitting at a desk away from the main group, is the teaching assistant for Sanjeev, who has prepared a copy of the text in Braille. Sanjeev requires a flat surface for reading Braille and for that reason he remains at his desk while the rest of the class is grouped around the teacher. His teaching assistant provides verbal reinforcement and description of the illustrations when needed. Once the children have discussed the text they return to their desks to work independently. The teacher works with one particular group of children of which Joseph is a member, leaving the rest of the children to get on with their work quietly. The general teaching assistant works with another table of pupils. Sanjeev is with his own teaching assistant.

Literacy was considered to cause some concerns simply because of the pace of the lesson. It is well documented that children with VI require more time than sighted children to achieve the same task. Problems sometimes arose when the Literacy Strategy introduced areas that Sanjeev had not yet developed in Braille. Service staff did not want to introduce the Braille signs and contractions in the

31

same order as prescribed in the Literacy Hour. The teaching of phonics posed another challenge as words in Braille are not divided phonetically. This meant that often Sanjeev was able only to follow the lesson verbally, with no possibility of learning through Braille.

The next lesson is science and the class is boisterous. It has been a wet playtime and the pupils have not been outside all morning. Again there are three members of staff present, only this time instead of the general teaching assistant there is an assistant who supports several pupils in the school at various times through the week. In this session she is timetabled to support Joseph, whom she sits next to. Again Sanjeev sits away from the main group of children with 'his' teaching assistant. The topic is 'Sound and Pitch'. The teacher has a box of instruments that he shows and plays to the class. Each time he demonstrates an instrument he gives it to Sanjeev to feel and play.

In the numeracy lesson (quick-fire mental maths), the teacher shouts out questions or writes out sums on the board for children to answer. A qualified teacher of the visually impaired (QTVI) supports Sanjeev in this lesson. His teaching assistant is out of the room preparing resources. The QTVI provides verbal reinforcement when questions are written on the board and tactile representations of fractions. Group work is then underway and the QTVI leaves Sanjeev for a while so that independently he can complete five questions. The QTVI wanders around the room assisting and talking to other pupils. The teacher checks Sanjeev is getting on. When there is nobody watching over him, Sanjeev fidgets and avoids completing the work.

Background

Pilkingston is a maintained primary school for boys and girls aged 4–11 years of age. The school is located within an urban area considered to be more seriously deprived than the national average (as stated in the LEA's education development plan). A higher than average number of pupils are entitled to free school meals and have formal statements of SEN; 8 per cent of the pupils are from ethnic minority backgrounds. Attainment levels at entry are average. Pupils attending the school live in a mixture of owner-occupied and rented accommodation (source of information: latest Office for Standards in Education (Ofsted) school inspection report). The school is situated within a large county LEA spanning both urban and rural areas. Across the LEA as a whole, the proportion of ethnic minority pupils within the county's schools is well above average and the proportion of pupils with special educational needs is high.

Two of the pupils within Pilkingston Primary School had visual difficulties and both had statements. Joseph was statemented primarily for MLD although he was seen by the visually impaired service on a monitoring basis. Relative to the class as a whole, Sanjeev was above average educationally, and he was particularly strong in numeracy. Sanjeev can be described as visually impaired without additional difficulties.

For Joseph, Pilkingston was his local school; for Sanjeev, the school was selected by his parents in consultation with members of the visually impaired team at the support service. Pilkingston was considered an appropriate choice by the service because of the school's positive attitudes towards pupils with special educational needs and because it had prior experience of VI. Previously, a family of children with difficulties, including VI, had attended the school. However, few of the teachers or teaching assistants working directly with Sanjeev and Joseph had direct experience of teaching visually impaired pupils. The general view expressed by the staff was that it had not been as difficult as they had originally anticipated.

> *Although I hadn't had prior experience of teaching children with visual impairment, I think you tend to think of all the negative things . . . they won't be able to find their way around the school . . . all the lessons are going to have to be so much different . . . it's got to have someone there who has got the skills that nobody else in the school will have [but] the school has already adapted and . . . it hasn't made a tremendous difference.*

[class teacher]

Sanjeev received 32½ hours per week support from a teaching assistant and five hours per week input from a QTVI and from a designated teacher (who had some training in teaching children with VI) from the LEA support service. The QTVI met with the teacher and sometimes the SENCO to devise a joint individual education plan (IEP); in addition the service developed its own specific teaching targets. The QTVI also supported Sanjeev in science and technology. Although teaching assistants usually carry out the bulk of preparation and prepare resources, generally it is the QTVIs who will develop the more specific or long-term resources such as models, mathematics aids or equipment for science or geography. The designated teacher had a support teaching role regarding Sanjeev.

Joseph was supported by a teaching assistant for eight hours a week and by a member of the learning support service for half an hour per week. He did not receive teaching support from a QTVI. His targets were school-based. When the QTVI did see Joseph it tended to be when he was withdrawn with his teaching assistant, or if school staff wanted to speak to her when she happened to be there for Sanjeev. Joseph was operating below the level of his peer group.

33

The teaching assistant had an IEP that she drew up in consultation with the outreach teacher who came into school for Joseph's other difficulties. Joseph received support both within the classroom and outside. The teacher was aware of Joseph's visual problems and was prepared to have work enlarged when required. The teaching assistant also took responsibility for enlarging worksheets and other material.

Pilkingston Primary School Mission Statement

Pilkingston Primary School seeks to create a happy, caring and secure learning environment. Parents, governors and teachers work in partnership to provide every pupil with a high quality education. All children are provided with opportunities, challenges and experiences to enable them to be confident and informed members of the community.

Pilkingston Primary School SEN policy

The SEN policy's stated objectives for pupils with SEN were:

- To support every child to reach their full potential.
- To provide full access to the National Curriculum wherever possible.
- To encourage every child to have a positive attitude to learning by developing programmes of study which proceed in finely graded steps.
- To provide a caring atmosphere in which children and teachers work together to promote the self-esteem and self-confidence of the child.
- To make and maintain good relationships with parents so that they can take an active part in the education of their child.

At the time policy documents were collected, the awaited revised Code of Practice for children with special needs had not been released. However, the school was aware that revisions to the current SEN policy might be required in light of the revised Code. Specific reference to this was given in the present policy. The school's SEN policy makes no specific reference to inclusion although reference is given to the fact that there are pupils with sensory impairments within the school and that such children have full access to the curriculum. Within the policy mention is made of 'integration'. The policy states that 'the school supports the *integration* of children with special educational needs into mainstream education when this is considered appropriate. We are aware of the need for careful planning of such integration, of close liaison with the special school or unit involved. Integration must be gradual including several visits by the child to school so that transition is accomplished smoothly' (emphasis added). As described in Chapter 2 (p. 11), there is a marked difference between integration and inclusion.

Environmental issues

The school was equipped to cater for the needs of children with mobility or physical problems including disabled toilet and shower facilities, and sloped access to school buildings. The playground area had recently been developed to incorporate shady areas, sensory and 'feely' plants and clearly marked playground games. Throughout the school, signs marking areas such as the library, toilet and staffroom were given in Braille as well as print. In the cloakroom, the radiators were guarded and Sanjeev and Joseph had easily located pegs close to the door. A careful audit of the school environment was conducted by a QTVI to establish where adaptations to the school building and grounds would be beneficial and to locate potential sources of danger.

Social inclusion

When observed in the playground, Sanjeev played with a particular group of friends. Joseph had difficulties with mixing socially with other children. He had fallen out with others on several occasions and had been called 'names'.

Both Sanjeev and Joseph were included in school trips. When Sanjeev was to go on a school visit, it was usual practice for the service to arrange to visit the location or event beforehand in order to make prior arrangements, e.g. for him to feel and handle exhibits and to locate potential sources of danger.

Concern was expressed by several of the staff interviewed that support staff could act as a barrier, preventing Sanjeev from socialising with other children. In the ever-close presence of an adult he was not at liberty to act as freely or naturally as his peers. It was considered an important part of the supporting role to try to pull back from him and not be over-protective. For Sanjeev it was considered an important part of social inclusion that he joined in with normal class routines such as sitting on the carpet when requested. Sanjeev had also been made the light monitor for the room, i.e. he was the child responsible for switching on and off the main set of lights in the classroom at the teacher's request.

We are always on the lookout for ways to make sure that Sanjeev, in particular, is included. It isn't always easy for him and it is our job to help things along a bit in that direction.

[teaching assistant]

Inclusion in the classroom

The experience of being in the classroom varied for both Sanjeev and Joseph depending on the subject, the teacher and various other idiosyncrasies. When in class, Joseph seemed to be part of the main group of children; he participated in the main activities, and seemed to be treated the same as the children who were not visually impaired. However, this did not appear to be so in the case of Sanjeev.

Sanjeev was positioned apart from the other children in the room; physically he appeared to be apart from the other children. When we observed the literacy lesson he was taught solely by the teaching assistant. We were informed that this seating arrangement was at the request of the designated teacher so that Sanjeev could have easy access to his bulky and quite heavy equipment. Furthermore, the teacher herself expressed concern about this arrangement because distancing Sanjeev from the rest of the group made it difficult for her to draw him into the lesson.

In that lesson there were also difficulties regarding Sanjeev's access to the curriculum area being addressed. There is no facility in Braille to format the page or to add pictures in a manner resembling the printed pages accessed by the other children in the room. Since it was page layout that was the focus of the lesson, the lack of congruence between learning to write and learning to Braille was problematic and of very little educational value to Sanjeev. This was an interesting lesson to observe because it is a very difficult area in which to include Sanjeev.

The science lesson was also interesting in that the teacher – due, we suggest, to his desire to include Sanjeev as a fully participating member of the group – singled Sanjeev out from the other children as the main demonstrator. Sanjeev appeared to enjoy the attention and the opportunity to play the musical instruments while the other children observed from a distance.

We suspect that these difficulties could be easily overcome were Sanjeev to have a more central seating arrangement. There was room in the class for him to have two or three workstations which he could use as appropriate to access the lesson more fully. Such an arrangement would have given him greater opportunity to mix with the other children and so promote his inclusion, rather than his integration.

Inclusion requires that the teacher takes 'ownership' of the child. However, this does not mean that additional demands are placed on the teacher:

> *Generally speaking the sorts of things that we would be asking a class teacher to consider . . . would be of use to all the children really. . . We are not asking them to jump through hoops of fire, we're really only asking them to write clearly on a blackboard, and when they've written on a blackboard not to say the title is on the board . . . or copy reams and reams off the board or whatever . . . but to verbalise what's on the board.*

[QTVI]

Alternatively, we would expect that the teacher should be able to articulate the attainment, targets and progress of the child, that records for the child with VI are physically kept in the same place as the records for the other children, and that the teacher meets and plans with the teaching assistant.

Additional skills training

Support for both Sanjeev and Joseph was provided through a mixture of withdrawal and in-class teaching. Withdrawal was considered essential to encourage independent access to the curriculum and to develop visual-specific skills such as Braille as well as other skills such as mobility and listening.

> *There are certain things with a visually impaired child that you need to withdraw for . . . Braille for example . . . If you are developing listening skills, you can't do that in a noisy classroom or even a classroom with normal work going on . . . But I don't like to withdraw.*

[service staff member]

> *You can't teach Braille in a classroom . . . You need the quiet and concentration in order to do it. You need to withdraw for skills such as touch-typing.*

[service staff member]

Withdrawing pupils was considered to be an exception because of the associated reduction in opportunities for the child to interact with peers, and because this practice acted to emphasise difference. The practice of withdrawing children was usually considered to be appropriate and to have value educationally. However, despite the stated view that withdrawal was an exceptional practice, it seemed to us that withdrawal was considered routine for many children throughout the whole school. Most staff supported this status quo, but there was one dissenting voice:

Inclusion, making sure that if it is full inclusion then the child has got to have full access to the National Curriculum in every way . . . Full participation, participating fully in all that goes on in the classroom as much as you possibly can . . . Inclusion means full inclusion and not withdrawing into little groups, to me that isn't it.

Wherever possible, withdrawal sessions at Pilkingston Primary School were organised so that their content coincided with the curriculum area being covered in the main classroom. Careful planning aimed to ensure that any lesson content within the withdrawal situation could be reinforced within the mainstream classroom itself. Support through withdrawal was timetabled on a rotating basis so that pupils did not miss out on the same subject every week. The 'withdrawal' area was placed centrally within the school and used by many children; because of this it seemed to be viewed by many staff as an extension of the classroom.

Sanjeev also received some support during the lunchtime period so that daily living and eating skills could be developed. Promoting daily living skills was felt to be an important part of Sanjeev's development and an area in which he lacked experience. Dressing was still slow and during a literacy activity it became apparent that he had no experience of making a cup of tea at home.

Communication

Communication between staff was achieved through a variety of systems, both formal and informal. A document was kept in the school so that the teacher had a written record of the targets set and details of support visits from the service. The teaching assistants were also expected to complete support records. Information on the system of communication and how it worked was somewhat conflicting. Some staff interviewed said that liaison was between the teacher and visiting teachers, whereas others said that communication tended to be between the teaching assistant and the visiting teacher, although opportunities could be found for visiting and class teachers to talk directly, if requested.

It can often be a case of . . . 5 minutes whenever you can.

[teaching assistant]

Training and staff development

Teachers working for the service are labelled either as 'specialist' teachers, i.e. they have a recognised qualification specifically for VI, hearing impairment or moderate learning difficulties, or 'designated' teachers, who have attended a university-accredited LEA 30-week training course. Designated teachers are not considered trained specialists but they do have an additional qualification for teaching children with special educational needs. Children with VI within the county may receive support from a QTVI or a designated teacher. Generally, children with more severe forms of VI – such as those classified as educationally blind – are supported by a QTVI. It was stated that a designated teacher can often adequately meet the needs of children with less severe forms of VI, whose access to the curriculum may require modification and adaptation through enlargement of print. In part, the decision to use designated teachers to support children with VI has developed because of difficulties in the recruitment of QTVIs.

Service staff reported that the teaching assistants working with pupils with VI generally had previous experience, but this was not the case of those at Pilkingston Primary School when they initially started in post.

I just had to learn as I went along . . . [This] is my first experience with a visually impaired child.

[class teacher]

All teaching assistants were entitled to go on generic county training courses but this was not built into their job description. Training through simulation situations for teaching assistants and school staff was offered. However, attendance at such training courses was poor. Teaching assistants were not prevented from going on the courses by the school: what prevented the teaching assistants attending was the lack of available places and funding from the LEA (they are not paid when on a training course).

At the time of writing, teaching assistants were given very limited specific training in teaching children with VI, although the aim for the future is to develop a full induction package.

I mean his learning support assistant is absolutely fantastic. It's sort of through her efforts really.

I mean she is really good . . . Thinking about this year I was a little nervous . . . so I chatted with the teaching assistant and she . . . calmed me down . . . She's great.

The teaching assistant is extremely good.

[class teachers]

39

However, it is considered good practice that teaching assistants receive quality training in the educational needs of the visually impaired. Farrell *et al.* (1999) state that: 'For LSAs who are likely to work with a specified group of pupils with identified disabilities, e.g. pupils with visual disabilities, some proven expertise in this area may be a necessary condition of the appointment. If it is not, then appropriate training should be provided immediately the post has been filled.'

The SENCO at Pilkingston Primary School organised a mini-appraisal for teaching assistants annually for them to discuss their job and professional development.

All teaching assistants employed by the generic support service were graded according to a banding system which related to the perceived needs of the child rather than the experience of the teaching assistant.

The support service offered some training to the school, typically upon entry and transfer. Schools were also provided with a pack of written information containing advice, strategies to use and guidance on literacy and numeracy. However, some staff expressed reservations about only receiving guidance through text.

> *I don't think paper-based [training] works because it is another piece of paper and it goes on the heap with other pieces of paper . . . I tend to do it informally [by talking to the people involved].*
>
> *[class teacher]*

Aside from training and advice from service staff, the school also received advice from subject consultants who occasionally came into school. One teacher reported that she had received conflicting advice from a mathematics consultant and the advisory teacher for VI. The consultant had suggested that formal recording was not something that staff should worry about whereas service staff had recommended that the visually impaired pupils should do the same as was expected of everyone else.

Points for discussion

- Pilkingston Primary School's SEN policy refers to integration, rather than inclusion. Is this important?
- What practices would you consider to be illustrative of an ethos of integration rather than inclusion?
- In what ways is the school working towards the development of an inclusive ethos?
- Many schools would claim to withdraw a child only when it is absolutely necessary. Is there a danger in making such decisions on a subjective basis?
- What would you consider to be the main characteristics of an *inclusive* classroom?

Class teacher, teaching assistant and visiting teacher, development session 1: Towards inclusive practice

This is the first of three sessions designed to support the professional development of the teacher, teaching assistant and visiting teacher as they work together to define and create more educationally inclusive practices:

- Session 1: Towards inclusive practice (this chapter)
- Session 2: Educational inclusion: towards a common language (Chapter 6)
- Session 3: Working in partnership (Chapter 7)

Each member of the team should have a copy of this session.

Towards inclusive practice

If you do not know your team members well, start here.

Have you experience of teaching or supporting children with VI? Have you relevant qualifications or training? Do you know a child who is blind or has low vision? Each member should answer in turn.

Task

Identify the strengths of the team, and the weaknesses.

Task

Allow a few minutes for each member of the team to explain his/her role in the educational inclusion of the child.

Otherwise, start here.

Each member of the team should take a few minutes to first define the term 'inclusion'. Then, as a group, write down any expectations, anxieties or concerns that you might have about meeting the needs of the child with VI in a mainstream classroom.

Inclusion is. . .

Expectations, anxieties and concerns

Task

With reference to the Pilkingston Primary School case study, identify barriers to achieving inclusive learning environment for Sanjeev and Joseph.

Task

Are there other barriers? If so, brainstorm to think of ways of overcoming the barriers.

Make sure that all three members of staff have:

- a copy of the child's IEP;
- a list of targets if the IEP is not yet available;
- a copy of the complete timetable.

Examine the timetable and targets:

Are there times when the child is timetabled to be out of the main classroom?

❏ yes ❏ no

If yes, is this for additional skills training, e.g. mobility, Braille, life skills?

❏ yes ❏ no

Does withdrawal result in the child missing out on the same subject every week?

❏ yes ❏ no

Does this also impact on opportunities for the child to meet targets?

❏ yes ❏ no

Can you rotate the main timetable or can visits be staggered so as to avoid the above?

❏ yes   ❏ no

How do you plan to achieve the targets?

What knowledge could the visiting teacher pass on to make the reinforcement of additional skills more effective?

Does bulky or specialist equipment for the child currently result in the child being separated physically from the rest or the majority of the class?

❏ yes   ❏ no

44

This is a common problem, but with some thought it can be resolved.

Currently, are there opportunities to encourage the child's development socially? (tick for yes)

- ❑ Plays and eats with peers
- ❑ Braille club for all children
- ❑ Attends school activities
- ❑ Visiting speaker on VI
- ❑ Many opportunities to interact with other children in class
- ❑ Is the child over-protected?
- ❑ Other

Do the teaching assistant and the teacher work in parallel for much of the time?

❑ yes ❑ no

How can the visiting teacher assist in developing a more cooperative way of working together?

It is important that the three of you have the chance to talk on a regular basis. In so many schools this takes place informally on a 'goodwill' basis. When can you get together? Are you fortunate in having a little time scheduled?

Task

Arrange your next meeting now.

4 Case study: St Elisabeth School

Entering the classroom

The classroom is filling with chatting children, fiddling with their bags and talking about the previous night's television viewing. The class teacher is writing questions on the board. While he is writing, a learning support assistant (LSA) from the LEA sensory support service is Brailling frantically on a Perkin's Brailler. Joanne enters the room with her friend and sighted guide. She sits at her desk and starts chatting to the children at her table before the lesson begins.

The Literacy Hour begins and the Year 6 class is asked to move and group around the big book in the middle of the classroom. Joanne moves with the rest of the class and listens while the teacher and pupils reads out the poem. The chorus is regularly repeated and Joanne joins in. She has memorised a large part of the text from previous readings throughout the week. While the class reads the poem, the teaching assistant remains at Joanne's table and writes up notes from the previous session so that the following support person to come in knows what has occurred. She also transcribes some of Joanne's Braille work for the class teacher to mark. The children in the class work together to develop a poem in the style of the one they have been reading. Joanne is an active member of the class and participates well.

The classroom is quiet. The children have gone to hymn practice. Present in the room is a teaching assistant from the sensory support service. She is working on a one-to-one basis with Joanne on some maths work which recent voluntary SAT tests have revealed are areas with which Joanne is struggling. Joanne does not miss hymn practice on a regular basis. She is a very bright child who is very much a part of the class. She concentrates hard during the session. The teaching assistant is explaining to Joanne how to go about reading tactile representations of Venn diagrams and how to measure angles. It is a slow and fiddly process. Joanne tries to make sure she feels the German film correctly to place a pin in the right place from which she can measure the angle. As she feels and counts the markings on the protractor, the pin falls out. She is unaware. Joanne offers an answer that is incorrect. The teaching assistant urges her to check her answer. Joanne feels once more and realises the pin is missing. She attempts the question again. This time her answer is right. In order to increase her understanding of the process and dexterity in doing so, the teaching assistant gives Joanne a series of angles to measure. While Joanne is getting on with this work, the teaching assistant writes up the procedure taught for measuring angles in the working file so that other support staff working with Joanne follow a consistent approach.

On another occasion, again during a Literacy Hour, Joanne is part of the group which is working with the class teacher. A teaching assistant is present but remains at a distance. The children are selected to read aloud sections of the text. Joanne follows and when requested reads a section from her Braille copy. The children are then asked to find the meaning of some of the vocabulary using a dictionary. The LSA passes Joanne her talking dictionary and she responds to one of the questions. It takes her a little longer than the other children to locate the words in her dictionary because of the processes involved in finding the word.

During RE, Joanne's class is asked to 'write-up in their books' the topic they have been discussing. The class gets on well. Joanne doesn't understand a section of the text. She asks her LSA for help. The LSA was not present in the initial delivery of the lesson as she was covering for another staff member who was ill. She encourages Joanne to ask the class teacher directly. Joanne feels her way round the room to the teacher's desk where the class teacher advises her.

Background

St Elisabeth is a Roman Catholic, voluntary-aided infant and junior school for boys and girls aged 4–11 years. The school is situated about five miles from the city centre and within a metropolitan borough of 'great diversity', incorporating inner-city areas which are disadvantaged and affluent suburbs (as stated in the LEA's education development plan). Pupils attending St Elisabeth typically live close to the school and a significant number come from homes in which there are social and economic difficulties. Attainment levels on entry are a little below average generally with an average proportion of pupils being eligible for free school meals (source of information: the latest Ofsted school inspection report).

St Elisabeth is Joanne's local school and her placement there was the decision of her parents. Joanne received almost full-time support from a team of teaching assistants and QTVIs from the LEA sensory support service. Academically, Joanne was one of the most able in the class. Voluntary SATs results showed that she was achieving better than average national scores.

Only one of the staff interviewed from St Elisabeth had prior experience of VI. One class teacher had taught a child with low vision in a previous school. All members of school staff interviewed initially felt nervous about having a blind child in the school; however, all stated that situation had turned out positively.

> *I was very worried personally because I have never had dealings with severely visually impaired pupils . . . [but] there has never been a problem.*
>
> *There was apprehension . . . you think what will your role be like, will you do the wrong things, say the wrong things. Having the support worker in the class as well, it is another strain . . . Having had her over the last three years, for two years, then it has been fine.*
>
> [staff comments]

The relationship between the service and the school was excellent, as the following comments testify.

> *[The service] just made everything go smoothly. There has never been a problem . . . The proof of the pudding is the fact that it works so well and if every service were to follow the model things would move a lot quicker . . . I do think that the way the service is run is absolutely tremendous. It is very efficient.*
>
> [head teacher]

> *The support has been great for her and it only works with that support.*
>
> [class teacher]

> *I think that the success depends upon the excellent way that the service in this LEA, the support service is run. It is excellent.*
>
> [SENCO]

St Elisabeth School considered periods of withdrawal for group or one-to-one tuition with a specialist teacher, classroom assistant or parent helper to be important and appropriate for many children. Support was usually provided in class although Joanne was withdrawn for some periods: mobility, additional skills training, or pre-tutoring for literacy and numeracy. Joanne was not taken out of the class at the same time every week so she did not miss the same class session each time. Withdrawal for Joanne was an opportunity to work on the development of specialist skills and did not take place as a means for remedial support.

There are still the odd times when I need to withdraw her to promote the inclusion . . . Sometimes we might have to use separate centres to do some mobility, that is all to promote inclusion.

[QTVI]

The nature of the provision for Joanne was established by the sensory support service and implemented with the full cooperation and collaboration of the school. The service was in possession of the class teacher's long-term plans, and additional work and planning was collected weekly so that resources could be prepared in advance and support provision planned. The support team made recommendations towards the IEP based around the class teacher's planning. Time to prepare resources and materials for Joanne to use was allocated in the timetables of the teaching assistants, for example during periods when Joanne did not require a teaching assistant. This way of working also provided a good opportunity for Joanne to interact and socialise with her classmates.

Sometimes the teaching assistant taught a small group of children that included Joanne; occasionally she taught the whole class. For instance, there were times when the teaching assistant took the class for PE, leaving the class teacher to support Joanne. This gave the class teacher an opportunity to work with Joanne and to better understand the nature of her needs, e.g. how to provide extra verbal input for Joanne during visual demonstrations.

Specialist equipment

In order to access the curriculum alongside her peers, Joanne made use of and had access to a variety of specialist equipment. She used a Perkin's Brailler, a laptop computer, a talking calculator, a tape recorder and specialist maths equipment such as a Braille protractor, ruler, metre stick and talking scales. Most of the equipment was kept in the classroom alongside the rest of Joanne's things so that she had independent access to it when needed. Where possible the equipment could be used with headphones to minimise disturbance to the rest of the class. Additional equipment such as 3D shapes and tactile material was kept at the service base and brought into school as and when required.

St Elisabeth School Mission Statement

St Elisabeth School aims to provide for the children of our Catholic community, an environment of faith and love in which the individual talents of each child are recognised to the full. The school aims to nurture, develop, guide and educate our children so that they are enriched and prepare to move forward with Christ in their journey of faith.

St Elisabeth School SEN policy

The SEN policy's stated objectives for pupils with special educational needs include:

- Providing opportunities to work towards the full cooperation of parents in identifying and meeting the needs of all children.
- To educate children with special educational needs as far as possible within the existing framework of the whole school, by promoting a positive self-image and positive attitudes from staff towards these children.
- To systematically review the curriculum for these children in order to ensure its accessibility and relevance to all pupils, in line with the National Curriculum.
- To provide opportunities for class teachers to discuss pupils experiencing learning difficulties and to provide in-service education and training (INSET) to have a common understanding.
- To acknowledge the value of and establish a working partnership with the external agencies.

The term *inclusion* is not mentioned within the school's SEN policy but reference is made to integration: 'Children with SEN are *integrated* into mainstream classes alongside their peer group. They are fully *integrated* at dinner times and break-times unless behaviour difficulties dictate other forms of arrangement' (emphasis added).

The organisation of the sensory support service

Almost all the pupils with VI in the authority are placed in mainstream schools. At the time of writing, one child was being educated out of the authority because of an additional medical condition, and another child who had initially been placed in St Elisabeth was moved to unit provision because of additional learning difficulties.

Usually the child is allocated a specialist QTVI and a key worker teaching assistant. The key worker is responsible for directly liaising with the class teacher to ensure lesson plans are obtained and that work is collected for adaptation. However, the child will also be supported by several other members of the team.

In part, this model of working developed because there were large numbers of part-time staff within the service, and each staff member needed to be fully aware of their own area of responsibility. However, the system evolved for a number of reasons and has several benefits. Severely visually impaired children requiring significant amounts of support can become overly reliant on a specific member of staff. By having various staff working with an individual child such difficulties might be avoided or lessened. In addition, this system of 'sharing children' provides an excellent means of on-the-job training as staff can talk and learn from each other. Furthermore, opportunities are provided to observe each other's working practices. All staff are required to develop a range of skills and expertise because they must meet a diversity of needs. This has the knock-on effect of ensuring the service has a bank of expert staff from which to draw.

Other benefits of this system are that the heavy workload associated with preparing large quantities of Braille is shared, and that teaching assistants have opportunities to develop their skills in particular subject areas.

Although some staff from schools under this service reported initial reservations about this way of working, it seemed to be well accepted once the school experienced the system in operation. The communication strategies within the service are well developed so school staff are well aware of who is coming in, what they are aiming to do and how they are going to work. School staff at St Elisabeth talked very positively about this model of working because of the benefits they perceived for encouraging Joanne's independence and because the system is managed well.

Environmental issues

The head teacher of St Elisabeth School in conjunction with the head of the sensory support service has sought funding from various means such as government grants and donations from local businesses to make the school 'environmentally friendly'. Additional facilities provided by the school for disabled students include a disabled toilet and a path suitable for children with VI.

Social inclusion

We observed Joanne's class being transported from the school to the swimming pool by coach. The coach was a lively place and the children were full of chatter. Joanne spent most of the journey in animated conversation with a group of her classmates, telling them about her favourite latest film *Scream*. Joanne goes to friends' houses for tea and is a member of the Brownies. There have been times when Joanne has fallen out with some of her friends and had reported they had been 'mean' to her. However, this was felt to be no more than would have been encountered by any other child of her age.

Inclusion in the classroom

Joanne appeared to participate fully in school life and in lessons, and to be highly motivated to achieve academically. In whole-class sessions she was positioned in the middle of the back row so that bulky equipment could be stored safely while still allowing her to be part of the main group. She moved to other spaces in the room when appropriate. She had a high level of support and in some ways this might equate to an overall level of education that was better than that received by her peers; the standard of one-to-one support was high, with teaching assistants having good subject knowledge and good teaching skills. We were of the impression that the presence of support staff for long periods of time meant that Joanne had fewer opportunities in class to participate socially with her peers. However, in her case, service staff took positive action to allow Joanne opportunity for social interaction. Joanne appeared to relate well to her peers and to have very good social skills.

Service staff felt that the introduction of the Literacy Strategy impacted on their ways of working. In order to promote inclusion in the Literacy Hour, it was believed that more pre- and post-lesson tutoring was required. This impacted on service timetabling. School staff who had taught Joanne prior to the introduction of the Literacy Strategy stated that Joanne had been able to operate well in English lessons without support but that this was no longer the case. In terms of the Literacy Strategy, one class teacher reported that Joanne did not have equal access to information compared with her peer group because pupils are frequently asked to carry out independent research requiring the use of a large number of sources. In numeracy, Joanne required extra time to develop her tactile skills for reading diagrams, charts and measuring angles etc. School staff reported that PE was one of the most difficult lessons in which to include Joanne, especially with regard to team games. Swimming, gym and dance presented few difficulties for the teachers although issues of safety were a consideration.

Additional skills training

Provision for the training Joanne needs in Braille, keyboard skills and daily living was achieved through a mixture of withdrawal and the mainstream classroom.

> *We have had her pouring liquid, you know say within capacity lessons . . . And you can easily transfer that to a cup of tea as she gets older . . . These things are ongoing in the classroom but they don't take over from curricular needs.*

> [class teacher]

The QTVI who supports Joanne was also a trained mobility officer and she took responsibility for that area within the early years and within school.

> *I do all the early years and in school. It is not a separate issue . . . it is about inclusion because it's an integral part of any programme. It is not something I take them out for all of the time. I may use PE.*

Within the service itself all the QTVIs and teaching assistants have taken an accredited module on orientation and mobility so they can support the trained mobility officer and also inform parents.

Communication

Effective teaching and learning for Joanne required good communication between all the staff involved with her education.

Communication was achieved in the main by informal mechanisms. Lunchtimes and after-school sessions were used, as no non-contact time had been made available. In spite of this, all staff stated that they managed to liaise informally with service staff. As the child progressed through the school, the new class teacher would consult with the previous class teacher.

The service had a documented communications policy that was reflected in the job descriptions of its staff. This appeared to be a key factor in the success of their programme. First, teaching assistants working for the service were expected to return and report to the service base at least three times a week; QTVIs reported on a daily basis. Secondly, communication was achieved through weekly staff meetings. Thirdly, communication was facilitated through the system of 'sharing children' that acted as a key mechanism for promoting exchange. Finally, there was a transparent and monitored system for writing up daily session notes. A lever arch file was accessible in every school, containing the service aims, ethos, contact details and recommendations towards the IEP as well as written reports of every support session. Each support session report contained a section for follow-up work that was anticipated. This promoted communication not only with service staff but also with school staff, as there was clear guidance that was easily accessible.

> *I want staff to know . . . why we are there. We are not just in there to support curriculum access, that is not good enough. I want them to know exactly what specific things they are doing on what, what the aims are.*

[service head]

Training and staff development

Apart from their own school-based in-service training programmes, St Elisabeth had welcomed the training and advice offered by the sensory support service. It was the opinion of most of the school staff interviewed that it was most effective to receive information verbally, but that it was important that written information was also available that could be referred to as and when required.

The support service had a policy of offering *individualised full school in-service training* for each child at entry or transfer, and the information given was updated each year.

> *The responsibility lies with the school, we are there to help schools, support schools, parents and the child firstly not to take a territorial view that it is our child.*

[service staff member]

The service had an ongoing programme of training and development for all members of the team. Targets for training were incorporated into the service development plan and also written into job descriptions. Every year, each member of staff was expected to design their own programme of training, and specify short- and long-term targets for their development. There was a minimum requirement for training.

Conclusion

With regard to Joanne being at St Elisabeth School, the message was clear. All those we spoke to suggested that her inclusion in the school was working well. Joanne was in the mainstream classroom for the vast majority of the school day, although periods of withdrawal were regarded as essential. This success might be linked to the support service and the systems provided. Capacity building in school and service staff was facilitated through INSET, assisted by carefully thought-out and justified support practices. The challenge for St Elisabeth was to embrace inclusion more widely, for all its pupils, and to develop whole-school policies towards this aim.

Points for discussion

- Identify the key factors that seem to have led to a very positive educational experience for Joanne.
- How would you distinguish between *integration* and *inclusion*?
- What are the advantages of having an effective support service for Joanne?
- Are there 'dangers' regarding effective educational inclusion for the school because of the existence of a good support service?

5 Case study: St Edward's CE Primary School

I feel totally supported, I feel totally comfortable with the situation . . . and what we are doing at the moment feels right . . . I don't think Sarah is any different to the others, I mean I feel I'm learning about each one of them day by day.

[class teacher]

Entering the classroom

There is hustle and bustle as children enter the classroom, slinging their bags on the floor. One child tries to cram books into his already overflowing tray. Chatter. The class teacher is busy organising the morning's activities. Once sorted, she commands quiet and the noise and bustle ceases. A maths test follows and pupils are given quick-fire mental mathematics questions. The teacher explains they will need to perfect their technique for the impending SATs. The pupils are quiet while the test is underway. The only noise comes from the far end of the room where Sarah, a blind pupil, is tapping out question responses on her Perkin's Brailler. There is a teaching assistant present in the room employed to support Sarah. She keeps her distance while the test is completed. The test is finished and the pupils go through the answers together. They discuss various ways of calculating the answer and strategies for jotting down the question if they are unable to tackle it in the designated time. Year 6 is of mixed ability and there is a wide range of performance on the test. The class teacher encourages the pupils to work on improving their scores and praises those for whom there has been improvement. Sarah has struggled, as have some of the other pupils around her.

The children are asked to put their things down and look at the board. The classroom has been organised in a U-shape with some children seated in rows within the 'U'. The topic is 'Area'. Time is running out and the teacher quickly draws a rectangle on the board with the measurements labelled. She points to the shape and asks the children how they would calculate the area and what the answer would be. The teaching assistant jumps into action. She hastily draws the shape for Sarah on German film, explaining what is happening as she does so. The pace of the lesson is fast. Some of the children quickly grasp the concepts, others struggle and the key points are reinforced. The teaching assistant guides Sarah's hand so she can feel and gain some understanding of the task. Area is then introduced and the teaching assistant explains in detail to Sarah what it means and how to go about calculating it. The children are given some questions on area to answer from the textbook. The class gets on. The class teacher wanders around the room assisting individual pupils; she also checks on Sarah and the teaching assistant. The teaching assistant mentions some of the difficulties and how she has gone about explaining the task.

After break, the children go into assembly, where school merit awards are given out and achievement is celebrated. Once finished, the children make their way back to the classroom. Sarah is guided by her teaching assistant. Not all the class return at the same time as some are engaged in various jobs associated with the assembly. It is time for literacy. As some of the class are missing the teacher asks individual pupils to read aloud extracts from film script they have been writing. The children enjoy reading. Some 'perform' using various voices for the different speakers. The teacher discusses each performance, picking out positive elements and discussing with the class why they were considered to be good. The children are then asked to market the film script they have been working on by writing a blurb about it. Strategies for doing so are discussed. Key words are written up on the board. Pupils get on.

The teaching assistant Brailles the words put up on the board for Sarah. Once Sarah is set on task, the teaching assistant pulls back to let her work on her own. Towards the end of the lesson, the class is invited to read their work aloud again. Sarah has a go. It takes her longer than the other children to read out her work but nobody minds. Once she's finished, the class motion as if they are going to clap. The class teacher gives the children a stern look and quickly takes charge, discussing the merits of Sarah's work. She has done well. It has taken some time for Sarah to get into reading but now she's on her way.

Background

St Edward's CE Primary School is of above average size and situated in a rural area. The number of children receiving free school meals is below average although the level of social and economic deprivation is above average overall. Most of the pupils attending St Edward's are of white British origin and only a small proportion of ethnic minorities are represented. The range of ability within the school is wide although overall, attainment is below average (source of information: the latest Ofsted school inspection report). The school had been identified by HMI inspectors as having serious weaknesses, and during the period of research a new head teacher was appointed. The school has a long history of provision for pupils with VI. The provision for pupils with special educational needs was considered to be 'good overall and for the visually impaired pupils it was very good' (Ofsted school inspection report). Until very recently the LEA's visually impaired service was housed within a neighbouring special school. The LEA has a strong policy of promoting inclusion of children with special educational needs in the mainstream and is very clear that the preferred option for any child is placement in a mainstream school.

The small group of children with VI at St Edward's had additional difficulties, and attended the school because they needed regular access to the resource base for VI. For these children, St Edward's was unlikely to be their local school (although it was for Sarah) and several used transport laid on by the authority to bring them to school. Being a centre for VI meant that having children who are blind with additional difficulties had become an accepted part of school life. It is worth pointing out that the additional difficulties of some of the children with VI are such that in many authorities they would be in a special school.

Together, the school and service worked in partnership to enable pupils with visual difficulties to 'share the educational experiences enjoyed by their sighted peers' (partnership agreement). A 0.5 FTE advisory teacher of visual impairment, three specialist teaching assistants and two lunchtime supervisors who had been specifically trained to work with children with VI were employed. All members of the VI team held additional qualifications in VI.

The VI team provided 'specialist teaching, experiences to supplement visually mediated activities, and oversee the VI pupils' safety' (partnership agreement). Pupils with VI might also receive specialist additional teaching in visually related skills such as Braille, daily living skills training and IT.

This welcome School/Service collaboration began several years ago, prospering through . . . goodwill . . . There is close liaison . . . The Service Manager . . . is available to . . . closely liaise . . . in promoting collaborative practice with class teachers . . . and all personnel . . . Working co-operatively with the Key teacher to modify classroom management . . . enable the pupil to take a full part in all activities . . . sharing in exchanging ideas.

(partnership agreement)

59

There was a designated room in the school that had been specifically designed for children with VI. This was fully equipped with blinds, supplementary lighting, contrasting work surfaces, floor covering, electrical sockets and tactile cues to assist orientation. Speech-accessible software was available on the computer and there was a talking microwave. Curriculum materials and equipment were stored within the room and pupils with VI had independent access to these. The room was used as a place for enhancing the additional needs of pupils with VI, for individual and group teaching, meetings and assessments as well as the preparation of materials and resources. Children from other schools travelled to St Edward's to use the resource base.

Sarah was at the lower end of the class academically, and struggled with some areas of the curriculum, particularly reading. She had timetabled tutorial sessions in the resource rooms which were 'very focused' (partnership agreement) and concentrated on the development of VI-specific skills or on the consolidation of learning. A great deal of time had been spent developing Sarah's reading and Braille skills and she was improving, albeit slowly.

Specialist equipment

- Perkin's Brailler
- Tactile alternatives
- German film
- Resource room and specialist equipment, e.g. talking microwave

Environmental issues

The school is equipped with a special resource room for children with VI. Displays throughout the school are accessible to children with limited functional vision and there is appropriate signing. There are steps in the school that can act as a barrier for some children, particularly if they also use a wheelchair.

Social inclusion

Sarah did not have a particular friend although she mixed better when in class. She was described as a 'clingy' child and quite dependent.

That's also something that we've got to address with Sarah, the fact that she can be very clingy with people, and it is teaching her the appropriateness of when she can do that or not. That's something I know that they are working on, particularly when she is out of the classroom on visual impairment work. And getting her to walk independently down the corridor and that sort of thing, so they are going to do a lot of work with her about that, particularly when it comes to Year 6 about the issues around . . . sex ed and that type of work. They are going to look at those issues with her before the Year 6s do sex education. And talk through those issues with her, that she has got to deal with, teaching her that she can't trust everybody, and it's not appropriate to be overly friendly to everybody.

[class teacher]

Sometimes I go into schools and you can look at what happens in the classroom and the children are very much included in the classroom, but when you look at what happens in the playground it's sometimes a different story. At playtime Sarah sometimes struggles but somebody will come to chat to her.

[visiting teacher]

Both the class teachers and the teaching assistant working with Sarah identified the need to develop Sarah's independence and this was related to the development of social skills. This aim was specifically built into her IEP. Strategies included the teaching assistant taking positive steps to back away from Sarah when she had understood the tasks and could be left to get on, and giving her a set quota of work to do independently within a set time.

What we're trying at the moment with Sarah is we're trying to get her less reliant on help from others . . . That is now on Sarah's latest IEP . . . She is getting into that sort of dependency culture type thing . . . We're trying very much for the teaching assistant to back off a bit . . . Telling Sarah you know the next part of the math's work . . . I'll be back in five minutes . . . That sort of thing and lengthen that time.

The teaching assistant also ran a lunchtime Braille club, which provided good opportunity for Sarah to develop social skills as she was expert and able to help others.

Sarah also joined in activities outside school for children with VI. Having access to other blind children was important for Sarah; it helped her to understand her condition better as well as providing extra opportunities to socialise.

Inclusion in the classroom

The extent to which teaching staff felt they had altered or modified their teaching style for Sarah varied, however all were aware of accommodations they could carry out to make their teaching more accessible.

I'm also conscious . . . of saying that child's name before answering a question . . . A couple of times . . . I've totally forgotten, I've meant Sarah to answer but using a visual cue rather than a sound cue. Then it has hit me you know . . . I try to make sure that the planning is done very early on.

[visiting teacher]

One class teacher commented that she was careful to ensure that Sarah had some knowledge of what had happened in class lessons when she had been withdrawn to the resource room. The teacher felt this was an important way of keeping Sarah up to date and it could also serve as an important means of revision for the rest of the class.

. . . when the situation happens you are very careful, you go back and you actually use it with the rest of the class as a revision session . . . so it's a worthwhile activity for them and at the same time you are bringing that person back in.

[class teacher]

It was apparent in some of the interviews that teachers were reflective and worried about whether what they were doing was right.

And sometimes I think am I getting this right . . . I don't want to go over the top, I don't want to over-include . . . you can over-include them in a lesson and therefore you are putting horrendous pressure on them because you are almost sort of demanding an answer from them.

[class teacher]

Some staff suggested that the introduction of the Literacy Strategy had imposed new issues in supporting VI pupils because the pace of the lesson was fast and there was a lot to get through. Sarah and other Braille users usually read more slowly than sighted children and 'keeping up' could sometimes be difficult. For Sarah it was thought that in some situations it was more productive for her to listen than to read Braille, as she would get lost and spend too much time trying to locate her place in the Braille text. On such occasions Sarah would then be withdrawn to read the text again at a later stage.

Additional skills training

Sarah had additional skills training in life skills, Braille and mobility for which she was withdrawn to the resource room with the advisory VI teacher. She was also learning to touch-type at a nearby special school for pupils with physical difficulties. The teaching assistant also spent some time reinforcing these skills. Generally, withdrawal was used as a time to develop important VI-related skills and Sarah spent the majority of her time in the mainstream classroom.

Mobility and being independent within the school were considered important by all staff and an issue for all concerned.

Communication, training and staff development

All staff at the school were experienced in working with pupils with VI and followed an ongoing programme of INSET training to further develop this. All members of the VI team held additional qualifications in VI. The team was considered very much part of the school and its members were encouraged to attend school-related training in addition to service-related training. The advisory teacher for VI attended many staff meetings at St Edward's as well as providing VI-related INSET. The specialist teaching assistant working with Sarah had attended several courses, all of which were organised through the service.

> *I've been on a lot of courses. I learned the Braille and I learnt mobility skills . . . I went on a two-day course for classroom support assistants that was very useful because they came from all over the country and you could swap ideas . . . you learn quite a lot from that. I went to see how examination papers were prepared . . . I went on . . . a literacy course . . . I'm going on one tomorrow on the literacy and numeracy hour.*

[teaching assistant]

The service had been influential in developing a course for teaching assistants working with children with VI in conjunction with other VI services in the region. The course was university accredited and teaching assistants were encouraged to seek accreditation if they so wished. All teaching assistants working for the service had to learn Braille. All members of the service – including those employed in St Edward's – attended training courses run by the service itself or by outside agencies, such as the Royal National Institute for the Blind (RNIB). The service had a developmental review scheme for all teaching and support staff through which individual and team needs were identified.

At St Edward's, the advisory teacher and teaching assistants attended weekly VI service meetings; IEP meetings were held each term. Weekly meetings were held between the advisory teacher and teaching assistants to plan curriculum differentiation and prepare materials. Strategies of support were discussed. Time for class teachers to liaise with support staff was limited and this often took place at lunchtime or during break.

> *I do a lot of talking with the support assistant and saying that's what we are going to do and she will say right I know we can do this with Sarah that will help . . . we can do it this way round, that sort of thing.*

> [advisory teacher]

The head teacher reported that class teachers were released once every half term to talk to the advisory VI teacher, to seek advice and discuss any difficulties, etc. At the beginning of the academic year the school introduced the use of a staff message book. St Edward's had a large staff and there were several visitors to the school. The staff message book was therefore considered as an important way of enhancing staff communication.

Points for discussion

- What are the advantages and disadvantages of resource schools?
- How can children with limited social skills who find mixing with other children difficult be encouraged and supported to become more outgoing and confident?
- In the vignette at the beginning of this chapter, why does the teacher give the children a stern look when they want to clap Sarah?
- Children with VI at St Edward's school are often withdrawn for specialist support. Comment.

6 Case study: Willow Vale School

I felt excited and a bit apprehensive . . . I felt slightly nervous . . . I thought, can I do this? . . . I am so happy that he has achieved so much because of the team . . . We have put so much into it not just for him but everyone.

[teaching assistant]

Inclusion is to be the same as everybody else . . . do the same as everybody else, curriculum wise and every other wise, as far as is possibly possible.

[class teacher]

Entering the classroom

Exercise! The reception children line up and march outside to the yard with the staff: a bilingual classroom assistant, a trainee teacher, a class teacher and a teaching assistant. Treading in line is Sumaja. Sumaja has low vision in conjunction with additional difficulties. She has a mild hearing impairment and physical difficulties, and moves around with the aid of a walking frame. The children stand in line at the back of the yard by the wall. Right children, jump! The children and staff jump across the yard. Hop! The children hop. The teacher puts some hoops on the ground. She calls out, 'Jump and find a hoop to stand in. Quick there's not enough for everybody!' Sumaja pushes her walking frame and jumps along with it. The teaching assistant jumps past her. Quick Sumaja. One pupil doesn't get there quickly enough. She is 'out'. Off they go again this time hopping. Sumaja does a mixture of hopping and jumping and rushes towards a hoop. One of her classmates grabs her, hurrying her along. The teaching assistant tells the child quietly to let Sumaja have a go on her own. Someone is 'out' again.

It's the Literacy Hour for Year 2 and there are three members of staff present in the room: the class teacher, a bilingual support assistant and a teaching assistant. The teaching assistant is there to support Suhail, a child with high myopia who needs support for his visual difficulties. All the children are seated on the carpet. The class teacher sits in front of a work stand on which she has placed a copy of a text. She uses a pointer to draw the children's attention when referring to vocabulary on a display board or words in the text. Suhail is seated at a table at the very edge of the carpet area next to 'his' teaching assistant. The teaching assistant has prepared a large copy of the text for Suhail, which she places on a reading stand. She also has a pointer which is identical to that used by the class teacher.

Together the class reads the literacy text assisted by the class teacher and teaching assistant, who use pointers to refer to the words on the copies of the text. The teaching assistant provides minimal verbal support and Suhail follows his copy at the same pace as the rest of the class. After reading the text through twice, the class teacher involves the group in discussion. She allows Suhail extra time to locate the required word on his copy of the text. The class teacher refers to the meaning of a related word within a different text, which she discusses with the group. This text has not been individually prepared for Suhail and the class teacher tells him to approach the front, go to the class work stand and have a good close look. Suhail participates well in the lesson.

Group work follows, and the class has been dismissed from the carpet area to get on with their work. Suhail's group is reading together. Each child has a copy of the book – Suhail's is the same except that the text has been enlarged to the appropriate size for him to be able to read it. The children take it in turns to read a section from the book. Suhail follows and reads a paragraph when it is his turn. His book is placed on a reading stand, which allows him to read without stooping his head. Staff members wander from group to group, talking to the children and keeping a watchful eye that they are on task and that none are struggling. The teaching assistant is working with another group of children as Suhail's group is progressing well. The class teacher approaches the group and pauses to listen to them reading for a while.

On another occasion, later on in the course of the research, Suhail's class has progressed to Year 3 and they have a new class teacher. The teaching assistant is the same member of staff as in the previous year. The class is grouped around the class teacher and computer. Suhail is seated on a chair next to the teacher. 'His' teaching assistant, together with another assistant, is busily preparing materials and organising the classroom. The teacher is explaining features of the keyboard to the class and demonstrating how to move the cursor around the screen, how to move down a line, enter text and use capitals and punctuation. The class teacher holds the keyboard close in front of the children and shows them the relevant key. She questions the group, 'Which one is the spacebar?' Suhail points, eager to demonstrate to his classmates his knowledge on the keyboard. The class teacher smiles and tells him to wait awhile and give the other pupils time to try to answer. She asks a different question, 'Which one moves the cursor down a line?' Suhail again points to the appropriate key. The class teacher laughs.

Literacy, Year 3! Christmas is approaching and the teacher has brought in a stocking bursting with secrets. The class is excited and tries to guess what is inside. All the children except Suhail are seated on the floor around the teacher; Suhail sits on a chair at the front by the reading stand so he is at eye level with the stocking. The teacher gives some of the pupils the stocking to feel and have a guess. What is in it? Marbles! Sweets! Presents! Some of the children seem fearful of the stocking and shy away from touching it. They can't think what might be in it. The teacher puts the stocking down and the children read a poem together about Christmas stockings. The teacher summons Suhail and he sits at a nearby table where the teaching assistant has placed a copy of the text on a reading stand. Both members of staff use identical pointers to highlight the words on the text as the children read aloud together. The pace of the reading is fast, and both the teaching assistant and Suhail struggle to keep up. Some of the children mouth the words, as if not entirely sure if they are reading correctly. The teacher asks the class to locate words with the vowel sounds 'oo', 'ee' and 'ay' in them. Pupils from the group are selected to approach the front and point to a word they think contains the sound given. Suhail's text has been enlarged and is spread over several sheets. The teaching assistant tries to flick over the sheets quickly so that Suhail can follow the word that the children have identified. Several pupils approach the front and are silent. They tentatively point to a word and await the response from the teacher.

Background

Willow Vale is an urban multicultural school situated on two sites. The nursery and reception are located on one site and the junior school on the other. All 25 children in the reception class were of Asian origin. Two children were visually impaired. Sumaja had several other complex additional difficulties and was described as having below average ability. Several members of the LEA learning support service supported her. She had a full-time teaching assistant and was visited by a QTVI and a specialist teacher who advised on her physical difficulties. Suhail had very low vision but was described as being 'quite a bright little boy'. He was supported by a QTVI who visited the school on a fortnightly basis.

Suhail received support from a teaching assistant for 15 hours a week but this was raised temporarily to 18 hours per week because of service staff shortages. This meant that Suhail had limited access to a visiting teacher. Through negotiation, it was established that he would receive regular visits from an advisory VI teacher once a fortnight. The class teacher felt that when there was no teaching assistant available, Suhail did not have full access to the curriculum. In her view, children with VI needed additional support for them to participate fully in the curriculum and socially.

> *. . . if you are going to have inclusion then the support has to be provided for that.*
>
> [class teacher]

The learning support service for Willow Vale also serves Pilkingston Primary School (Chapter 3). As was documented in Chapter 3, the head of the learning support service and area coordinator for VI (who was also the designated advisory teacher for Suhail) were interviewed in conjunction with the project. At Willow Vale, we also interviewed and spoke informally with three class teachers and two teaching assistants. Due to unforeseen circumstances such as staff illness and unscheduled school meetings, we were unable to formally interview the head teacher or SENCO. Nevertheless, we did speak with both these members of staff during meetings to arrange access and in the staffroom during break.

There was a strong emphasis on group work within the school. Both Sumaja and Suhail were witnessed working in various groups with different members of staff. Sumaja often worked with several members of staff, on rare occasions working one-to-one with a teaching assistant. The teacher believed that children with SEN should be in the classroom as much as possible, and that she should adapt to cater for them.

> *I do like Sumaja to join in. In a lot of the class activities . . . it may be just her as a person but she is very determined and she does like to join in everything.*
>
> [class teacher]

Both Sumaja and Suhail reportedly did not like being taken out of the classroom.

> *She won't concentrate when she is out . . . She will play up a bit.*
>
> [class teacher]

> *We don't take him out because he doesn't like it . . . He didn't want to be taken out so he was silly and he just wouldn't respond.*
>
> [class teacher]

We witnessed Sumaja's lack of cooperation during a withdrawal session in which she was taken out to work with another girl on a literacy activity using a worksheet, making some use of CCTV equipment provided by the service as a low vision aid. Sumaja was non-cooperative and difficult to keep on task. We were told that Suhail was now never taken out of the room except during assessment.

Specialist equipment

Suhail had his own whiteboard as he had great difficulty reading from the class board. Both children made use of enlarged and modified print and had their own workbooks with wide lines etc. They had been provided with CCTV and had their own reading stand. Training for staff in the use of CCTV was said to have been minimal.

I think I got fifteen minutes.

[class teacher]

We were explained how to use it, but it was rather rushed.

[class teacher]

There were mixed views about its benefits.

We don't tend to use the CCTV a lot because we find it alienating.

[teaching assistant]

On occasions, the specialist equipment for Sumaja and Suhail was used generally in the classroom in an attempt to encourage them to be more accepting of additional specialist equipment. For example, some of the other children would use Suhail's reading stand when he was not using it, and the CCTV had been used for classroom demonstration purposes.

Environmental issues

At the time of writing only minor adjustments had been made to Willow Vale's built environment regarding matters of safety. As the relationship between the school and service develops it is to be expected that opportunities will arise enabling additional appropriate adaptations to be made. However, since Sumaja and Suhail have low vision, and are not educationally blind, major adaptations are not anticipated.

Social inclusion

It seemed that neither Sumaja nor Suhail were less socially included than their peers because of their visual impairments, either in the classroom or in the playground.

Inclusion in the classroom

We consider that both Sumaja and Suhail are educationally included. The class teachers took responsibility for the children with VI to ensure their participation, and the class teachers and teaching assistants worked very much in partnership. The child was always part of the main lesson. The class teacher often allowed the child extra time to assimilate information which may have had a positive knock-on effect for some of the other pupils in the class. With regard to Suhail, the class teacher was conscious that the pace of the lesson could be too fast and she sometimes paused for a short while to give him a chance to think. Suhail was also encouraged to move close to the board in order to access information and the teacher used a signal to alert him when it was time to start another activity. Sumaja's teacher and teaching assistant had developed a strategy to inform the teacher whether or not she was keeping pace during whole-class instruction. Quite simply, the teacher would nod at the teaching assistant who would then inform her whether or not the child was keeping up with a smile or a shake of the head. In both the reception year and Suhail's classroom, the teaching assistants provided occasional input during whole-class activities to supplement the input from the class teachers. This helped to ensure that the child was participating in the class and not following a separate, one-to-one lesson with a support assistant. This view was backed up by reports given during the interviews.

> *The class teacher has been superb. Whatever I have suggested she has been willing to take on board ... An awful lot depends on the teacher. [This child] is very well included.*

[QTVI]

Literacy was reported to be one of the subjects that school staff believed was the most difficult in which to include Sumaja or Suhail. First, there was concern about the pressure to produce materials just for the visually impaired child and the subsequent effect that providing such materials can make to the physical inclusion of the child within the room.

70

[Preparing the resources], we have to do that after school. They have to make a copy for Sumaja but that can separate her out.

[class teacher]

Secondly, the teaching assistant talked about the text with Sumaja on a one-to-one basis. The class teacher found this distracting, but believed it was not something that could be easily avoided since Sumaja needed her own copy and could not maintain the pace of the majority of children in the class.

I find it difficult because Sumaja obviously talks about her book and I'm talking about the big book that the rest of the class use. And there is a noise and the noise level goes up a bit. But you can't stop Sumaja talking because she wants to talk about it. But she also wants to be part of the class lesson; so that is what we find difficult.

[class teacher]

The Numeracy Hour was also considered to be difficult for Sumaja. As it was very practical in the reception class, this was more because of her physical difficulties than her visual impairment.

Additional skills training

Very little additional skills training was available to Sumaja or Suhail at the time the research was conducted.

Communication

Verbal communication between visiting advisory staff and the class teacher was stated to be difficult because of restrictions in time, and because visiting staff were not always available during break and lunchtimes. Service staff communicated through written information and wrote a report of every visit made to the school and classroom before leaving the school.

The teaching assistants reported that they did get an opportunity to liaise with the visiting teachers. However, some staff members felt that time for communication should be formally organised and timetabled.

Communication between teaching staff and teaching assistants was achieved through both formal and informal means. Staff would meet weekly as a group to discuss the timetable and planning for the following week. Informal talk and discussion between the class teacher and the teaching assistant took place during after-work hours.

Training and staff development

Details of training opportunities and staff development in relation to the service providing support for Sumaja and Suhail were documented in Chapter 3. None of the staff in Willow Vale had previous experience of children with VI prior to Suhail and Sumaja, and some stated that the initial training and advice from the service had been limited.

> *When Suhail came [originally, the service] did come and give me a little bit of advice about what to do . . . I do feel that I could do with a bit more training.*
>
> [class teacher]

> *The only real training I can honestly say that I have had has been this year. Last year we were using our initiative, on the hop really, finding out what works and what doesn't work.*
>
> [class teacher]

It was stated that teaching assistants should have training before they start working with the child. Sumaja's assistant had been interviewed and selected by the class teacher rather than through the service.

> *They actually need training before they start the job . . . The current teaching assistant has done a good job. But she had no training at all before she came to the school . . . so she is actually learning what to do with the children and learning what to do with the visually impaired children. It is really very busy . . . I don't get a lot of time to tell them.*
>
> [class teacher]

> *At the moment the training I have is by talking to other helpers in the class . . . and the help from the visiting advisory teachers. I would love to go on training courses. You learn more.*
>
> [teaching assistant]

> *I am going on a VI course and I think it's two days . . . but to me it is not enough, basically it is not enough.*
>
> [teaching assistant]

Both the teachers had applied to go on the training organised by the LEA (see p. 39 for further details of the training available from the LEA).

Some staff reported that they had had to push for service staff to come in and support them. They were keen to gain advice and information as to how to assist their pupils in the classroom. One or two of the staff had undertaken their own research through reading and by visiting a special school for pupils with visual difficulties in order to get an alternative view of how other schools catered for the needs of children with VI.

Points for discussion

- Explain what is meant by teacher ownership of the child.
- How would you define *inclusive* teaching?
- One class teacher with little initial specific guidance from a specialist service has successfully established inclusive practice within the classroom. This was achieved through her own reading and research on the subject of inclusion and VI, the development of a clearly defined relationship between herself and the LSA and subsequent input and suggestions from service staff. Discuss.
- In what ways can provision given by the service be viewed as a vehicle for facilitating educational inclusion at Willow Vale?
- What should be the role of the service regarding facilitating educational inclusion for visually impaired children?
- 'Inclusion must be regarded as a never-ending process, rather than a simple change of state, dependent upon continuous pedagogical and organisational development in response to pupil diversity. It means of course, that deep changes are needed and inevitably, they take time' (Ainscow *et al.* 1999: 137). Discuss.

Class teacher, teaching assistant and visiting teacher, development session 2: Educational inclusion: towards a common language

By the end of this session you should have:

❑ Developed a shared understanding of the following terms:
  • Disability
  • Impairment
  • Integration
  • Inclusion
  • Teacher ownership
  • Educational inclusion
❑ Made comparisons between the three case studies in order to develop a joint understanding of the process of the educational inclusion of the child with VI who you are in the course of educationally including.

Educational inclusion

Task

Read the following text carefully.

An educationally inclusive school is defined by Ofsted as one 'in which the teaching and learning, achievements, attitudes and well being of every young person matters'. Significantly, for the first time, Ofsted has equated the terms effective schools and educationally inclusive schools, 'effective schools *are* educationally inclusive schools. This shows not only in their performance, but also in their ethos and their willingness to offer new opportunities to pupils who may have experienced previous difficulties'.

The difference between *integration* and *inclusion* is highlighted in the case studies. The term *integration* can be associated with the medical model of disability in which problems in education are considered as residing with the individual. Hence, that individual must adapt, fit or integrate with the already existing system of the school. *Inclusion*, alternatively, is hand-in-glove with the social model of disability. The social model implies that disabilities are as much products of the environment, attitudes and institutional practices as they are products of the impairment itself. By altering attitudes and institutional practices schools can do much to reduce barriers to access and participation (Booth *et al.* 2000). *Inclusion*, therefore, involves a different approach whereby attempts are made to resolve difficulties within the school, rather than accepting that difficulties reside solely within the child, because of his or her disability. It has been argued that developing a language for inclusion is important, as when educational problems are ascribed to pupil deficits, this can conceal barriers to learning and participation, and hide opportunities for the development of school policies and practices for all children (Booth *et al.* 2000: 13; Ainscow *et al.* 1999). Moreover, as other writers have argued, inclusion 'requires a detailed and precise definition, for otherwise there is a danger that schools can claim that their provision is inclusive when the opposite may well be the case' (Feiler and Gibson 1999).

Task

With reference to the text, discuss the following statements and questions with your team members.

Once a child is admitted to a school, it is an equal opportunities issue whether he or she can participate fully in the learning and 'life' of the school. It is your job to make this happen.

With reference to the second extract and the case studies, explain the difference in meaning between the terms impairment and disability.

Impairment

Disability

To which model of disability do the following terms belong?

SEN children	❑ medical	❑ social
Children with special educational needs	❑ medical	❑ social

How do you refer to this group of children? ....

VI children   ❏ medical   ❏ social
The visually disabled   ❏ medical   ❏ social
Children with visual impairment   ❏ medical   ❏ social

Task

There are under-represented groups of children within primary schools who are vulnerable to the risk of marginalisation, exclusion or underachievement. As a group, vulnerable children encompass a wide variety of circumstances, for example children with a disability, travellers' children, sick children, poor attenders, and so on. However, in particular, vulnerable children tend to live in areas of high social deprivation, come from bilingual ethnic minority families, or are classed as having special educational needs or a disability.

When you hear the word inclusion, which group of children do you think about?

Children with special educational needs ❏
Vulnerable children   ❏
Statemented children   ❏
Children with additional needs   ❏
All children   ❏
Other?   If so, please define   ....

With reference to the case studies (Chapters 3–5), define the term *teacher ownership*.

```
Teacher ownership is . . .




```

Work together to define your team's understanding of the term *educational inclusion*.

```
Educational inclusion is . . .




```

Why is it important that Ofsted should equate an effective school with an inclusive school?

Task

Complete the following table.
Fill the dot if you consider the characteristic to apply to the school regarding the inclusion of the child or children with VI.

	Pilkingston School	St Elisabeth School	Willow Vale School
Integration	◯	◯	◯
Environment appropriate	◯	◯	◯
Social inclusion	◯	◯	◯
High degree of outside school support	◯	◯	◯
Teacher ownership	◯	◯	◯
Teaching assistant:			
One-to-one	◯	◯	◯
Small groups	◯	◯	◯
Whole class	◯	◯	◯
Partnership with teacher	◯	◯	◯
Impairment	◯	◯	◯

Disability	O	O	O
Educational inclusion	O	O	O

Task

Write down a list of words that you consider characterise the process of inclusion at the current time for the child with VI in your class.
In what ways do you want to move your practice forward?

Task

Arrange the time of your next meeting.

7 Working in partnership

Introduction

The purpose of this chapter is to understand the ways in which the teacher, teaching assistant and visiting teacher can work together. In particular, this chapter illuminates how teamwork between the teacher, teaching assistant and visiting teacher can be encouraged in order to arrive at a situation whereby the staff involved are 'pulling in the same direction', with the shared aim of creating an educationally inclusive learning environment for the child with VI. This chapter begins with an explanation of different modes of working for teachers, teaching assistants and specialist teachers – all well documented in recent literature (e.g. Balshaw and Farrell 2002).

This chapter moves forward with a discussion of the meaning of partnership in the context of working with others in the classroom and an exploration of the term *teacher ownership*, and in doing so draws upon the findings of the ESRC research. Scenarios of teaching and learning practices observed during the research are discussed. Finally, staff development session 3, 'Working in partnership', is located at the end of this chapter.

Models of working together

'The more that teachers are constrained to work individually, deploying routinised and somewhat narrow expertise, the less likely they are to develop the flexible problem-solving strategies which will enable them to respond appropriately to the diversity of learners in their classrooms' (Clark *et al.* 1999: 158).

In the main, discussions on the role and practice of teaching assistants focus on ways in which they can become a barrier to the child's participation in lesson activities and how teaching assistants can promote or facilitate the child's inclusion in the classroom. Simply, when a teaching assistant works on a one-to-one basis with the child for much of the day, opportunities for social inclusion – and importantly, inclusion in the lessons that are taking place in the classroom – become limited. This way of working has sometimes been termed *velcro*, because it appears that the teaching assistant and child are stuck together. Instead, ways of working that involve other children or that connect the child directly to the main lesson are preferred, e.g. small group work, or the teaching assistant having prior knowledge of the content of the lesson and a clarity of purpose of his/her role in the delivery of the lesson. Thus, for effective inclusion to take place, the role of the teaching assistant needs to be more diverse and 'closer' to that of the class teacher. This also is 'hand-in-glove' with the notion of teacher ownership, whereby the class teacher views the child first and foremost as his/her responsibility, i.e. the expectation is that the child will be part of the main activities taking place in the room. In order to achieve teacher ownership, the teacher and teaching assistant must work in partnership to meet the needs of the child, as the easier option of working separately with minimal communication is pushed aside as unsatisfactory and contrary to the spirit of inclusion.

Lessons from the research

Regarding the ESRC research on the inclusion of children with VI in mainstream schools, we found that there were two distinct groups of schools; the first group being schools in which in-house provision and support was valued, and where a relatively large proportion of resources was allotted to special educational needs. In these schools, staff had taken responsibility for SEN – they did not assume that the responsibility for children with difficulties lay with expertise solely from outside the school. For instance, attitudes typically encountered in this group of schools were:

> *This idea of getting her more integrated into the classroom with less dependence . . . You are part of this group now and I am including you from the minute I see you until the minute you go home.*

[class teacher]

> *It's always been basically the same; we've always worked within the classroom.*

[teaching assistant]

> *Sometimes I like to withdraw them, not on a regular basis.*

[visiting teacher]

I see my role as facilitating in class, because you know, and they are included, they want access to the National Curriculum.

[class teacher]

In the second group, by contrast, the schools rely heavily on expertise from outside the school. The dependence on outside help seems to result in less responsibility being assumed within the school. This issue appears to be about ownership of the difficulties, which children experience through the school and also through the class teacher. For example,

The danger that you can get . . . is that the class teacher doesn't take ownership of the child, and because there is . . . support there, they feel they can delegate the teaching responsibility . . . and don't see the child as theirs.

[service staff member]

We found that where there existed a culture of commitment to special educational needs and inclusion, there tended to be positive views about the nature, quality and direction of the provision. Where this internal commitment was lacking, we found that there was more reliance on external support, rather than partnership with the support service and staff. It should be of no great surprise, therefore, that school culture or ethos towards SEN and inclusion filters into the activities taking place in the classroom. *Teacher ownership* of the child with VI, in the sense we have defined it, tended to be observed more frequently in schools showing more commitment to the inclusion of the child.

Service staff often stated that they wanted the class teacher to take responsibility for the child and to develop teaching methods that were responsive to the child's needs. For instance, consider the following comment regarding barriers to the development of educationally inclusive practices in schools made by one of the LEA officers interviewed:

The big one is probably resources . . . The other barrier is attitude of mainstream staff and there is a perception being perpetuated . . . that special needs are a specialist problem, and therefore if you have a child with special needs you need a specialist intervention [all the time].

[LEA officer]

The importance of parental views in maintaining a separatist approach to the use of specialist support was also alluded to:

[A] barrier is with parental expectation, often parents look to specialist provision, only specialists can do it.

[head of service]

81

The comments of a head of service might also illuminate our understanding of this point:

Anxiety of staff and parents . . . I don't think the staff barriers are because they don't want to do it, it's anxiety, lack of confidence in their ability to make it work and anxiety about resources.

However, in the face of conflicting tensions, fast-paced lessons and the ongoing developing of mainstream staff expertise, we found that, with a few notable exceptions, service staff did not prioritise responsibility for the professional development of class teachers in relation to the effective education of children with VI in the mainstream. An impetus for services to provide more specific guidance to teachers and teaching assistants might lead to opportunities for developing an ethos of teacher ownership of children with VI (and more generally for children with special educational needs as a whole) that is commonplace in many schools.

During the research project, we found the following were indicators of successful partnership between the class teacher, teaching assistant and visiting teacher.

The roles of each member of the team were considered as skilled and varied:

I had to learn the Braille quickly so it didn't take me very long. Now, I used to do . . . do shorthand many years ago and I think that helped because I understood why there were the contractions and the short form. And they were very very similar, the contractions, the short forms and the shorthand to the Braille. So possibly I learnt it quicker than some people would because of that. Every morning before I went to work I used to do about 15 minutes, just because you need to do it daily you know, otherwise it doesn't go in.

[teaching assistant]

It's so dependent on the quality of the support that's provided, because if I'm honest really I don't have to do that much.

[class teacher]

The class teacher has been superb. Whatever I have suggested she has been willing to take on board . . . An awful lot depends on the teacher.

[service staff member]

The visiting teacher made it a priority to disseminate specialist knowledge to class teachers and teaching assistants:

I mean we can't do our job without it [providing training] if we're not all singing from the same tune. So especially . . . in secondary, which I know you are not looking at, but you would be making sure that every single member of staff has got that advice, and there may not always be time to do that. When they have their Ofsted it will be picked up on and that helps with the less supportive subject staff who don't take note of the child's individual needs. So that gives us, all that has really given us more credibility . . . And again, it is the same in primary, so it is easier in primary. Very much easier but the success does depend on schools taking responsibility themselves, we are there to help schools, support schools, parents and the child.

[head of service]

Formal time was designated for communication between the visiting teacher, class teacher and teaching assistant:

I do a lot of talking with the support assistant and saying that's what we're going to do and she will say right I know we can do this with Sarah and that will help . . . we can do it like this and that sort of thing.

[class teacher]

The teaching assistant was viewed as belonging to both the school community and the service for visual impairment:

We are an inclusive school, we have staff meetings which are for everyone, we have INSET for everyone and we don't delineate whether a child's got special needs or not, or whether staff are employed by a service or not, we are a community and that's how we run.

[head teacher]

Opportunities existed for teaching assistants to meet with and observe other teaching assistants:

The SSAs [specialist teaching assistants] are expected to come back at least three times a week to report; that is what we do and that is expected. We call that informal communication, it is daily ongoing communication . . . But the other important way of communication is by having some training days as a whole service. And the other big communication is staff meetings. We have them every week, after school, four till six and everybody is expected to attend, SSAs included.

[head of service]

Quality staff development and training for teaching assistants was in place:

Recruitment is difficult. And recruitment of well qualified people is difficult.

[head of service]

Our biggest problem is training ... there's a huge shortage of skilled people out there and when you advertise there's a lack of response which is worrying. Not as many teachers are going into support service work because the government agenda hitherto has been discouraging that sort of ...

[head of service]

We are having real problems recruiting people who are sufficiently skilled and qualified and that ... has a knock-on effect for the inclusion agenda because whilst we may be willing and parents may wish, if we can't get the staff to service the needs of these children, support our schools, then we are sometimes forced to look elsewhere, against our wishes.

[head of service]

Typical scenarios observed during the research

Scenario A

Joanne (St Elisabeth School) was working with one of her teaching assistants in the classroom while the rest of her class were at hymn practice. Joanne ordinarily enjoys hymn practice, as she does most other subjects, but every other week she misses part of singing to work on specific skills. In this session, the teaching assistant had targeted areas which caused difficulty for Joanne during a voluntary SATs test. The withdrawal session is used to practise using a protractor, reading tables, and scanning tactile diagrams for information. Measuring with a protractor and reading tables and charts is a slow arduous process and Joanne needs more time than her classmates to learn and develop her skills in this area.

Comment: Inevitably, if a child receives additional support during the normal school day then s/he must miss out on some other aspect of school life. Judgements such as this are made routinely and reflect the status afforded certain activities and subject knowledge. The above example is typical in that a compromise has been reached, whereby the child receives extra input for a subject given high status, while not always missing out on the activity afforded lower status.

Scenario B

The teaching assistant presents the charts in a number of formats. When using the protractor to measure angles, Joanne and her teaching assistant discuss different ways she could use her equipment. Practising these skills assists

Joanne to compete equally with her peer group who are able to practise skills such as chart reading more often as they come across them in magazines, school wall displays etc.

Comment: Considering educational inclusion as an equal opportunities issue might provide a way forward. Issues of equal opportunity relate to the social model of disability, as the onus for the success of the child is passed to the school, or school staff, rather than poor performance in a subject being accepted as a function of the child's inability.

> *I was a bit anxious, I suppose, at first because I didn't know what it entailed. But in actual fact . . . she has got a visual impairment and it's quite severe but it doesn't really impede her very much in anything because we don't let it. It is a case of equal opportunities.*
>
> [class teacher]

Scenario C

Nathan is a much younger child. He is withdrawn for regular periods with a qualified visiting teacher of the visually impaired. In the session observed, Nathan and his visiting teacher are also practising tactile skills and chart reading. Learning how to interpret tables and find information is a slow, lengthy process for Nathan and it takes a great deal of concentration. Nathan is withdrawn from his classroom to a quiet room in the school. Periods such as these ensure that Nathan can keep up and participate in the classroom alongside his peers.

Comment: Because of the importance of hearing in enabling access to the curriculum for children with VI, providing a quiet environment in which the child can distinguish sounds and information efficiently and easily is imperative.

Scenario D

Oliver is a reception child with low vision. During a Literacy Hour, the teacher directs the class to sit in the carpeted area at the front of the classroom. A teaching assistant is present in the room. She is there for the benefit of all the children and for the first half hour of the lesson pops in and out of the room preparing materials. The class teacher begins the lesson by reading a poem. Oliver is seated right at the front of the room directly in front of the reading stand on which the large font text is placed. Very basic and very clear pictures surround the text. When talking about the pictures the class teacher periodically instructs Oliver to go to the text and have a good, close look. She also reinforces any reference to the print with detailed verbal instruction. After reading the text together, the children are given different activities to do in groups. Children are given a variety of worksheets to complete. Oliver is provided with an enlarged copy of the worksheet. The worksheets for the whole class are clearly printed in large text. Oliver sits at a table with other children and the teaching assistant takes responsibility for the learning of Oliver and the other children on that table. She does not sit next to Oliver and gives him no more attention than any of the others sitting there.

Comment: This is a good example of teacher ownership in the first part of the lesson and also shows a typical supporting role for the teaching assistant. The teaching assistant is able to teach a small group of children. Again, this is representative of the means of working in many schools.

Scenario E

Sarah is a Year 6 pupil who has low vision and additional learning difficulties. During the Literacy Hour she sits at a desk near to the children, who are all seated on the carpeted area next to her LSA. She has her own enlarged copy of the big book but the pictures haven't come out well on the photocopier. The class teacher reads and discusses the big book with the whole class. The support worker reinforces what the teacher has said and helps Sarah to keep up with the rest of the class by turning over the pictures appropriately and pointing to the individual words. However, because the teaching assistant is talking to Sarah she misses out on some of the whole-class discussions. Some of the class talk is centred around the illustrations which Sarah cannot access as her individual copy does not sufficiently depict the pictures. The teaching assistant provides verbal descriptions of the pictures and, after the whole-class instruction has finished, gives Sarah the original copy of the big book to look at.

Comment: This scenario illustrates the importance of thorough preparation of materials for the lesson. The teaching assistant tries to make amends, but the child is denied access to the curriculum for much of the time. The importance of careful planning on the part of the teacher and teaching assistant is also highlighted.

Points for discussion

- Why is it important that the teacher should take ownership the child? After all, another adult might be being paid to support the child, perhaps on a full-time basis.

- If you work with others in the classroom, how would you classify the types of ways you work with each other?
- Regarding your school, consider the following indicators of successful partnership between teachers, teaching assistants and visiting teachers:
  - ❏ the roles of each member of the team: the visiting teacher, the class teacher and the teaching assistant are considered as skilled and varied;
  - ❏ the visiting teacher makes time to disseminate specialist knowledge to class teachers and teaching assistants;
  - ❏ formal time is designated for communication between the visiting teacher, class teacher and teaching assistant;
  - ❏ the teaching assistant is viewed as belonging to both the school community and the community of the service, responsible for VI;
  - ❏ there are opportunities for teaching assistants to meet with and observe other teaching assistants;
  - ❏ quality staff development and training for teaching assistants is in place.
- Scenarios A to E all illustrate dilemmas facing teachers on a daily basis. Comment on each of them.

Class teacher, teaching assistant and visiting teacher, development session 3: Working in partnership

By the end of this session you should have:

- Learned something useful from your team members about teaching and learning with regard to the child with VI.
- Developed an awareness of each other's roles as being skilled and varied.
- Considered the role of the child's peers and parents in strengthening the quality of the learning environment for the child.
- Developed a lesson plan in which an educationally inclusive learning environment is achieved, as you teach in partnership.

Working in partnership

Task

Select a lesson scheduled for next week that you would like to teach in a renewed and strengthened partnership.

What National Curriculum content is covered?

What are the aims of the lesson?

Date and time scheduled for this lesson.

Task

With the selected lesson in mind, what resources, materials and equipment will the child with VI require in order that s/he can participate fully in the lesson?

Resources, materials and equipment required.

Task

Plan the physical location of the child in the room.

If you have not done so already, devise a way of working for the child with VI so that s/he has ready access to specialist equipment and resources, but is never physically separated from other groups of children in the room.

Task

Develop the repertoire of teaching skills for the teaching assistant. Sometimes the teaching assistant will teach a small group of children and occasionally she teaches the whole class. As a teaching assistant you might feel apprehensive about taking on roles usually associated with the class teacher. You have a different role to the teacher and an important one. Not everyone will feel comfortable about taking a whole class, especially if until now you have worked solely with the child you are there to support. If this is your experience, then attempt something less ambitious – after all you do not have to 'kill all birds with one stone'. There is no requirement that you should be a whole-class teacher. You could work with a group of children including the child with VI, or with a different group of children. Aim to do something that you have not tried before as this is a good way to help the child develop independence, while also allowing the teacher to learn more about the child's learning needs so that s/he can take ownership of the child.

Decide what you will do and ask for advice as to how you might be most effective.

Task

Below are selected indicators of teacher ownership. Plan these into the lesson. Can you think of others?

    The teacher:
- ❑ Uses the child's name
- ❑ Checks that the child is on task
- ❑ Questions the child in whole-class lessons
- ❑ Works with the child in a small group
- ❑ Marks the child's work
- ❑ Keeps records for the child in same place as records for the others
- ❑ Other ....

What is the role of the teaching assistant when the teacher questions the child with VI in a whole-class instructional context?

What is the role of the teaching assistant when the teacher works with the child with VI in a small-group instructional context?

Task

Are there any tips that the teaching assistant can give the teacher about the child's learning needs? (For example: Do you use special symbols? Does the child exhibit particular mannerisms if stressed? What are the child's strengths and weaknesses in this subject area?)

> Tips for the teacher.
>
>
>
>
>
>
>
>
>
>

Task

Add opportunities for the child to reinforce additional skills to the plan.

> Decide how you will go about this together.
>
>
>
>
>
>
>
>

Task

Add an element of peer tutoring and support to the plan, e.g. paired reading.

> Brainstorm for peer tutoring and support activities.

Task

Can you think of ways of increasing the strength of the partnership between the parents of the child with VI and the school?

> Ideas for strengthening the partnership with parents.

LESSON PLAN   Title .... date and time ....

Team members ....

NC content and level

	Teacher	Teaching assistant	Child's peers	Child with VI	Time
Activity 1					
Activity 2					
Activity 3					
Activity 4					
Activity 5					

8 Developing inclusive practices

Introduction

The purpose of this chapter is to help non-specialist teachers and teaching assistants with responsibility for a child or children with VI. It relates closely to the previous chapter, 'Working in partnership' and between them, these chapters provide the knowledge and know-how required to enable a child with VI to participate in the classroom as fully as possible. This chapter is divided into two parts: the first examines the purpose of an additional curriculum; the second part focuses on teaching and learning in the main classroom and on the delivery of the main curriculum (the National Curriculum) and is usefully divided into three sections: children who learn through print, children who learn through touch and a section with tips that are applicable to all children with VI. A staff development session intended to be used independently by class teachers or teaching assistants is located at the end of this chapter.

The purpose of an additional curriculum

The purpose of providing an additional curriculum for children with VI is to enable the child to develop independence. Fully sighted children learn much through observation and imitation. Children with severe or profound VI require sustained teaching to learn many of the skills that fully sighted children learn with little input.

If you have ever observed a baby acquiring mobility, curious to learn, experience and explore you will have seen how s/he makes full use of all five senses. First, the baby might try to sit with support, then to sit unaided, then roll, crawl and finally walk. As the child becomes familiar with the surroundings s/he will grow in confidence, eager to explore that little bit further. Sight is a powerful enabler of typical child development.

Young children with severe VI have to learn to negotiate their environments with little functional vision (and in the case of a child who is totally blind, without sight). The home or school environment for these children is more limited, more contained and less stimulating than is the case for a child who is regarded as having normal sight; exploration might feel too dangerous and takes sustained effort and concentration. Young children who have very limited functional vision sometimes exhibit autistic characteristics or repetitive actions, such as continuous rocking, because of the self-limiting nature of their environment; however, with careful support and given time they can learn to 'widen their horizons' and become independent, while characteristics normally associated with the autistic spectrum or with serious disability often fade away. The earlier the need for additional support is identified and supplied the better will be the prognosis for the child.

Children with VI need to learn how to move around independently, how to dress, tie a shoelace, put on a coat, and how to clean and generally care for themselves. A blind child at the upper end of primary school – especially if s/he has additional difficulties – may still require support in putting on his/her coat before going 'out to play'. Many young children who are blind might begin school without the basic skills of using the toilet, self-feeding and dressing, particularly if the child and parents have received little support from specialists in a position to pass on useful know-how. Learning to do essential daily tasks such as these requires sustained effort and time in a supportive environment. Furthermore, some children might have grown accustomed to having 'everything done for them' and be reluctant to change this status quo.

Like children who are classified as blind, children with low vision might also require training in additional skills depending on the nature of the sight difficulty. It is worth pointing out that some children might find that their ability to move around independently depends on the weather that day. As Stone (1999) points out, a child who finds exposure to light problematic might be able to move around the playground freely when it is cloudy but be unable to see on a bright sunny day; this can cause some confusion among staff who have not been properly informed. Other children may be classified as having low vision but have a degenerative condition whereby they will eventually become blind. These children need special attention to help them cope with their impending loss of functional vision.

Additional skills training is supplied by the service for the visually impaired or equivalent, e.g. service for the sensory impaired or generic service for children with special educational needs. Usually the training will be provided by a qualified teacher of the visually impaired. It is a requirement that a qualified mobility officer supplies mobility training. Children with severe or profound VI might require two or three sessions a week with a mobility officer. Children with low vision may also receive additional skills training, but usually the extent of this training will be far less than for a child who is severely or profoundly visually impaired. Specialist teaching for children with VI is a skilled role, and many qualified teachers of the visually impaired have extensive experience and training (although this does vary considerably).

I mean it depends what they need, I mean obviously a lot of the job is sort of assessing vision to start with, seeing what their functional vision is, what their vision in school is, how they are using it, how they can better use it. How you can promote the vision they have got and then you are obviously working on how they can use that to access the curriculum, I mean it's all part and parcel really.

[visiting specialist teacher]

It is necessary to recognise the importance of the child receiving input from specialist teachers. Enabling the child to make the best use of his/her functional vision takes time, and although an initial assessment is essential and helpful, it is only with time and continued input that the teacher can become fine-tuned to the child's needs. Furthermore, for most children their eye condition will not be stable and their functional vision will change over time. Providing additional skills training – mobility and orientation, tactile awareness, and daily living skills which might also include learning Braille or learning Moon (a less complex, non-visual means of communication than Braille, often used with children with additional difficulties who could not cope with learning Braille) – should be considered as an issue of equal opportunity, as enabling the disability, perhaps, to become an impairment over time.

It is important to point out that no attempt is made in this book to provide a typical development profile for a child with VI; it encompasses such a wide range of conditions and degrees of severity that it is impossible to provide a profile that would apply to the majority of children. Moreover, such a profile could lead to misunderstandings as it would be unlikely to capture the developmental characteristics of any child that you might have in mind as you read this book. You might find it helpful to learn more about the child's condition(s): go to the RNIB website (see Useful addresses), which is an excellent source of information and also allows you to download fact sheets on many conditions and syndromes relating to VI.

Reinforcing the additional curriculum

I think it's about use of support assistants, if the child needs mobility then, the majority of our children that need mobility would have some sort of help as well from support assistants. I choose to work with the child and the support assistant. Which you know, I do a lot, so that the support assistant can carry on that training when I am gone. So that the child can practise skills throughout the day, throughout the week, not just when I am just going in, so I am transferring my skills really to the support assistant. In some schools the support assistants are then able to sometimes pass on skills to the class teacher, if the opportunity arises.

[visiting teacher]

Sometimes I go into schools and you can look at what happens in the classroom and the children are very much included in the classroom, but when you look at what happens in the playground it's sometimes a different story. I think it needs to be a joint venture between the class teacher, school and ourselves, because at the end of the day the child belongs to the school, she is their responsibility, but most definitely we can look at ways to talk to the child about what are appropriate forms of behaviour . . . because most of the children, we've known them since they were quite young, you can sit down and have a chat about worries, or how to initiate a conversation with somebody, what you think is appropriate and maybe what's not, and how do we deal with it, so I feel that you can actually be quite honest with a lot of children and say what's right and what's wrong, and what you don't do . . . but I try to work with the school and find out what they would be doing for a child who has difficulty in the playground or difficulty with socialising. It's not just because they are visually impaired . . . So I think we've got to look at what they would do as a school to try and work together really, and hopefully they wouldn't view it as being our problem. . .

[visiting teacher]

One of the most helpful things a teacher can do is to provide opportunities that can enable children to reinforce the skills they are developing with a specialist teacher. For example, encouraging mobility, tactile awareness and life skills. In our research we identified many ways in which additional skills were reinforced by the teacher or teaching assistant.

Mobility

- Asking the child to fetch or return the register.
- Asking the child to take messages to other teachers in other parts of the building.

- Making the child a room monitor, e.g. light monitor.
- Giving time before school for the child to use a walking machine.

Tactile awareness

- Providing as many real objects as possible in class for illustrative purposes. These can be touched by the child with VI but can also enliven the lesson for the other children.

Life skills

- Making sure that at lunchtime the child eats alongside peers, with or without a support assistant. (Sometimes children with VI need more time to eat lunch than their peers and to accommodate this, schools organise for the child to eat with younger children, who also need more time. This can mean that the child misses many social opportunities to mix with peers and it is a practice that should be avoided.)
- Making sure that the child plays outside at the same time as peers.
- Establishing a lunchtime Braille club available for all children to join.
- Organising visits, e.g. from Guide Dogs for the Blind.

Making use of home–school links

It is very likely that the visiting teacher will have a good knowledge of the child's family circumstances and will have developed a close relationship with the parents. Making use of this already established relationship might prove helpful to teachers wishing to strengthen the relationship between school and home.

> *And other support in terms of how they cope, the family may have concerns about David, social skills, social life, independence, so I do feel that part of my role is actually to talk to family, and empower the parents to take on board the responsibility for really to be supportive in any areas of concern.*
>
> [visiting teacher]

Teaching and learning in the main classroom

The second part of this chapter considers how the teacher can adapt to accommodate a child with VI in the main classroom.

Enabling access to the curriculum [lessons and social activities] to the same level as the others by adapting resources or teaching methods for him to do that, take part as fully as possible . . .

[visiting teacher]

Advice is given regarding children who learn through print, children who learn via other means, and other ways to facilitate educational inclusion in the classroom. While it will be necessary to work in partnership with the teaching assistant – and possibly a visiting teacher – much can also be learned from talking to the child and taking his/her views into consideration.

Children who learn through print (low vision)

Many children with low vision will benefit from having access to enlarged text and materials. Some of the strategies for producing these for children with low vision can be used when preparing material for the whole class. Materials provided in large print for the child with VI may also be used for demonstration purposes when addressing the whole class.

Children with low vision may also make use of low vision aids (LVAs): the benefit of these is that they promote independence. By being encouraged to use LVAs, children can learn to develop their own strategies for accessing independently the curriculum and information outside school such as bus timetables. A significant proportion of children with low vision, however, are reluctant to use LVAs because they feel stigmatised. Teachers can help to overcome this by taking opportunities to use the equipment with the whole class. The appropriateness and use of LVAs will, to an extent, depend on the age of the child; however, LVAs have been used with children as young as three years old.

Using the guidelines provided for adapting and enlarging text will be beneficial for children with low vision. However, the requirements for an individual can vary and not all the 'rules' might apply. For example, children with a severe loss to their field of vision are likely to have a small working area of vision and enlarging print means that they can actually see less when they look at the page. Guidance on the best way to enlarge print for a particular child should always be sought from a QTVI who knows the child concerned.

Adapting paper materials: general guidelines
- Use a print size and font appropriate for the individual child. Most children with VI prefer the fonts Helvetica or Arial and font sizes within the 18 to 24 point range (precise guidance on font size for the individual child should be sought from a QTVI).

- Materials should be printed in bold with 1.5 or double line spacing.
- Use a paper with a matt surface – avoid shiny paper as this results in glare.
- Lower case letters are easier to read than CAPITALS and avoid *italic* and ornate fonts.
- Clear contrast should be used: black on white paper, white on black or black on 5% green tint. Colour should be avoided but where used should provide a good contrast to the background.
- Where photocopied materials are used, darkening the contrast control may help.
- Page design should be clear – illustrations, pictures, tables, graphs may need simplifying and modifying.
- Illustrations should not be physically very close to the associated text.
- Scanning materials into a computer helps as this enables adaptation by manipulation of font and layout.
- The time required for children with VI to respond to worksheet or written tasks is likely to be more than that usually required by most children with good sight.

(Adapted from Arter *et al.* 1999.)

LVAs

While 'normal' sight is unlikely to be fully restored, using LVAs can make a significant difference to the child's functional vision. If you wear glasses take them off for a few minutes and see what difference that makes to your ability to function. If you do not require glasses, borrow a pair, preferably from someone with a strong prescription. The difference in your functional vision with and without glasses will not be the same as for a child with low vision, however, you will get an idea about their benefit. Furthermore, as Mason (1998: 4) points out, 'it is important to realise that LVAs are not just for reading, but instead they are individualised learning tools which extend the children's visual environment providing options for visual independence during and after school hours'.

The following are examples of LVAs to aid vision:

- Hand-held and stand magnifiers.
- Hand-held and spectacle-mounted telescopes.
- Overhead projectors (OHPs).
- Closed circuit televisions (CCTVs).
- Appropriate lighting.
- Colour filters.

- Reading stands.
- Computer packages to adapt text.

Guidance for encouraging the use of LVAs
- Introduce use at an early age.
- Allow children to personalise the aid with stickers.
- Use the aids for 'fun' tasks (such as board games, dot to dot, reading CDs, recipes) as well as academic work.
- Give children praise and encouragement and highlight improvements in work when an LVA has been used.
- Give status and value to the aid.
- Encourage families to play a role in promoting LVA use.
- Provide awareness training for peers.

(Adapted from Mason 1998)

Given the benefits stemming from the use of LVAs, it might come as some surprise that many children show reluctance to use them. It is important to realise that the child might be in a 'denial' phase regarding their sight and might require counselling from a professional with expertise in working with children with low vision (Mason and McCall 1997). Others might simply feel self-conscious or embarrassed. I was reminded of this recently when a friend's nine-year-old boy became distraught because he was told he needed to visit the optician – he did not want to wear glasses. We live in an age when, more than ever, body image is extremely important to many people. When taking a psychological rather than functional perspective, children's reluctance to use LVAs becomes readily understandable.

Mason (1998) suggests that children are more likely to accept their use of LVAs if they are able to observe others using them and if they can share their experiences with them. For example, CCTV can be used for more general classroom purposes such as during demonstrations, examining mini-beasts, bugs or looking at photographs brought in by pupils.

The findings of a comprehensive research study on LVAs are reported in Mason (1998). As well as confirming reluctance by many children to use LVAs, she also identifies insufficient knowledge by staff and children about their use as a key barrier to the educational inclusion of children with low vision. Training for the child should begin with the simplest format, the slowest speed and have the most orientation clues (for full guidelines see Mason 1998).

The use of some LVAs presents certain educational difficulties for the child, which teachers and teaching assistants should be aware of and take measures to overcome. Stand magnifiers do not allow reading and writing at the same time, they impede the speed of reading, create shadows and can cause head and neck pains. They cannot be used while typing. Some of these problems can be alleviated by:

- The installation of suitably raised desks.
- Suitable lighting.
- Use of other LVAs at appropriate times.

Telescopes are often heavy, can cause loss of orientation and objects might be difficult to locate. With distance telescopes, the field of view will be too small for the child to access television. Knowledge about the use and effectiveness of LVAs can therefore have important implications for practice.

It is recommended that children and staff update their training regularly in order for skills to be improved. Mason (1998) advises that *for each LVA* staff should be able to:

- Perform very simple tasks such as looking at stationary objects.
- Know how to hold the LVA correctly for near and distance viewing.
- Find the target and fix it in the field of vision.
- Follow a stationary object with the eyes.
- Follow a moving object.
- Understand the best lighting conditions for the child.
- Know how to provide the greatest contrast.
- Maintain the equipment.

Training on the use of LVAs may be available to you: ask a specialist teacher of the visually impaired or a specialist teaching assistant for advice. Make sure you know how best to use lighting.

Children who learn through touch

Some children will learn both through print and through an alternative form such as Braille; others will be limited to learning through touch. Although Braille is the most common method used, some children might require a simpler alternative such as Moon. Unless the child is totally blind, it is of extreme importance that s/he is provided with the optimal lighting conditions. This will be unique to each child and should be discussed with the visiting specialist teacher.

As a class teacher you might not wish to become an expert in the use of Braille or Moon (although some teachers choose to become so). It is important, however, that class teachers and non-specialist teaching assistants develop an awareness of the alternative communication methods. For instance, there are valid educational reasons for the class teacher to develop an awareness of Braille, since there are significant differences between learning to read through print and learning to read through Braille. Braille is not phonological in the sense that it cannot be broken down into phonemes, and the order of process of learning to read in Braille differs from the National Curriculum guidance for reading through print. This means that the child will not always be able to access information by Braille and may need to rely solely on sound. Furthermore, there is no facility in Braille for elaborate formatting of the page and teachers need to take heed of this when planning lessons in which page format is important.

In addition, a child might be in the early stages of learning Braille, while the majority of his/her peers have developed functional reading skills. This situation is not unlike that experienced by slow readers or dyslexic learners, and similarly requires careful attention to classroom practices so that the child has equal opportunity of access to the content of the curriculum.

Furthermore, in our experience, we found that children who learn through Braille (or Moon) appreciate the effort and gesture of a teacher who learns a few words and uses Braille (or Moon) from time to time.

Most children who use Braille will begin to learn on a mechanical Perkin's Brailler. They might later transfer to an electronic Brailling machine. In addition, many children who learn through touch will also be taught to touch-type. Some are supplied with computers and have access to specialist packages for the visually impaired.

Other ways to facilitate educational inclusion in the classroom

This section is intended to be helpful in developing the educational inclusion of all children with VI. Educational inclusion can also be enabled by:

- Using appropriate teaching methods.
- Specialist equipment.
- Appropriate classroom layout.
- Working in partnership with others in the classroom.
- Teacher ownership.
- Facilitating opportunities for the child to develop socially.
- Giving special attention to Literacy and Numeracy Hours.

Guidance on teaching methods
Provide verbal description:

- Read or verbalise when writing on the board during whole-class teaching.
- Use a black pen on the whiteboard (low vision).
- Refer to children by name.
- Use tactile representations and real objects.
- Organise good listening conditions.
- Give pupils time to formulate responses and complete tasks.

Following these guidelines can improve significantly the quality of learning experience for the child with VI. Simple as they might sound in theory, in practice achieving these conditions can prove more problematic. We know that many teachers tend to make limited use of children's names, and it is also good practice to state the name after asking a question rather than relying on visual cues.

I'm also conscious . . . of saying that child's name before answering a question . . . A couple of times . . . I've totally forgotten, I've meant Sarah to answer but using a visual cue rather than a sound cue. Then it has hit me you know . . . I try to make sure that planning is done very early on.

[class teacher]

A common concern of many commentators on education is that talk in the classroom is very often dominated by a discourse of control and classroom management. In general, relatively little time is afforded to discussion of curriculum content. In such classrooms, children with VI will be at a disadvantage. Even when this is not the case, it is very likely that the use of visual methods for curriculum delivery will predominate. After all, 90 per cent of the information that fully sighted people receive is through sight.

I'd try not to place too much emphasis on things that I've written down, when we are talking and I suppose I always make sure things are repeated quite often . . . When he puts his hand up then I always ask him as soon as I . . . can because that is one of the things we are trying to encourage him to do . . . I suppose it's not a particularly natural thing for a blind person to do to . . . attract attention. I try and avoid being too visual . . . although you've got to cater for everybody not just him . . . I try if I'm using something visual to try and find some equivalent . . . [And I] make sure I repeat . . . anything that's written on the board.

[class teacher]

Not style so much as just making sure that he is in the best place and has the appropriate things to look at and use, the actual style of teaching I don't think I've had to change . . .

[class teacher]

I don't treat her differently except . . . I am more aware now . . . If I have got a coloured background I see the teacher of the visually impaired. I either enlarge or I ask J . . . but she does exactly the same as the others.

[class teacher]

Providing sufficient information by other media (usually sound but also using touch) for the child to have full (and not intermittent) access to the curriculum is an acquired skill that requires careful consideration, reflection and practice to become routine and second nature.

When the predominant mode of access to information is via sound, then information exchange needs to be fully audible otherwise important information is lost and the child is denied equal opportunity of access to the same curriculum as his/her peers. This means that it is particularly important that children are quiet when someone is talking to the whole class. Furthermore, the use of participatory teaching methods and group work – which are encouraged as a means of facilitating social inclusion, in addition to promoting a deeper understanding – tends to result in noisier classrooms. There are contradictions facing the teacher regarding teaching children with SEN. Methods for dealing with the pragmatics of inclusion include peer tutoring and pre- or post-session tutoring.

Modification of teaching practices and style in order to include the child with VI is achievable and can be very effective. Furthermore, attention to the details of the guidance should be of benefit to the other children in the class, some of whom might benefit from more time to think about their responses, from clear materials that are easy on the eyes, from receiving sufficient information through sound as well as sight, or who may find the use of real objects more stimulating.

Specialist equipment

Bulky equipment and equipment requiring electric power can prove a serious limitation to where the child can be seated, which can result in separating the child from his/her peer group. A number of examples of good practice that help to tackle this issue were observed during the course of the research.

❏ The quickest and most cost effective way was to move furniture and reorganise the classroom.

❏ Alternative strategies included offering the child a number of workstations: a position near the front of the class for board work, a position with peers for class work and an area close to another peer group for using CCTV. The child was encouraged to be responsible for his own learning and to move to the appropriate position for the appropriate activity.

❏ In another instance a school had purchased a trolley complete with power sockets for the CCTV. This not only meant the CCTV did not take up valuable space in the classroom but also meant it could be easily transferred when required by the child or for classroom demonstration purposes.

Classroom layout

A child with VI – especially if educationally blind – will require time to learn to negotiate walking around the classroom. Regular changes to classroom layout should be avoided (perhaps changing classroom layout just once during the school year). This is contrary to advice on good practice concerning classroom layout for non-visually impaired children.

Displays

Guidance for displaying work:

• Display work at an appropriate height. For blind children this means hand height, for the child with low vision this means eye level.
• Work should be mounted on a contrasting background, e.g. white on black.
• Use clear, large print.
• Do not use shiny or laminated materials as these result in glare which will make them inaccessible for some children.

(Adapted from Arter *et al.* 1999)

Working with others

Developing a working *partnership* between the teaching assistant, teacher and visiting teacher, and *teacher ownership* is considered essential for the effective educational inclusion of children with VI (as for other children). These concepts have been discussed at some length in Chapter 7. Working together in this way will also do much to facilitate the child's social inclusion.

Other opportunities for strengthening social inclusion

The following are examples of ways that the class teacher can enable the development of the child's social inclusion in the school:

- Ask the child to be the light monitor.
- Send the child with messages to other parts of the building.
- Establish a lunchtime Braille club.
- The teacher should learn a little Braille.
- Goal Ball Club. This is a 'football-like' game for children with VI that can also be played by fully sighted children.
- Raise awareness of VI in school.
- Peer tutoring.
- Use of participatory teaching methods.
- Use LVAs with all the children.

Furthermore, careful planning and consultation is required to enable the child to take part in all activities, school visits, swimming etc. with the proviso that it is safe to do so.

> *We provide after-school activities, but the special needs children tend to go home in transport, so they can't stay after school.*

> [head teacher]

Enabling access to out-of-school activities and activities for the school holidays can be encouraged by teachers developing strong relationships with parents, and via the specialist visiting teacher and service.

> *We've had quite a lot of visually impaired activities, where Dominic's brought to the front of it all.*

> [class teacher]

> *We've had quite a lot of visually impaired activities in school. We've had a listening week, we've had the guide dogs coming pretty often. We've had the visually impaired bus, all sorts of activities like that.*

> [class teacher]

The National Literacy and Numeracy Strategies

All the services we encountered during the course of the inquiry had developed excellent guidance on teaching methods in specific lessons such as the Literacy and Numeracy Hours. The advent of the National Literacy and

Numeracy Strategies has placed new challenges on those with responsibility for children with VI. Both the strategies have a detailed structure, which supports teachers in the daily planning and delivery of lessons. The task for those working with pupils with VI in an inclusive classroom is to ensure that practice continues to meet the specific needs of the partially sighted and Braille users, while ensuring they are fully participating members of the group.

Several staff stated that the introduction of the Literacy and Numeracy Strategies, with their detailed structures, had caused difficulties in responding to pupil diversity. Service staff commented that both had impacted on their ways of working. In order to promote inclusion in the Literacy Hour, it was believed that more pre- and post-tutoring had been required. This had impacted on service timetabling as both subjects were targeted for support. In one service the introduction of the Literacy Strategy had led to an increase in statementing.

The National Literacy Strategy

Modifications to allow youngsters to participate in the Literacy Hour, as it was, meant very often the child ended up doing almost separate work. So, we actually developed guidelines for schools who had got our youngsters and ways of modifying the Literacy Hour.

[service member]

It is actually the Literacy Hour that we find hardest.

[class teacher]

In particular, it is important to adapt the lesson to allow for the mismatch between learning to read through print and learning to read through Braille. Some schools had found getting Braille versions of the required texts or the big books problematic as the following quotation illustrates:

I find [the literacy] difficult because she talks about her book and I'm talking about the big book that the rest of the class use. And there is a noise and the noise level goes up a bit. But you can't stop her talking because she wants to talk about it. But she also wants to be part of the class lesson; so that's what we find difficult.

[class teacher]

Some schools had developed useful links with the National Braille Library and others used the services of prisoners who Braille. Should you require further information on the Literacy Hour, we recommend Rogers and Roe (1999).

The National Numeracy Strategy

The National Numeracy Strategy recommends a direct teaching approach involving interactive oral work and an emphasis on mental calculation. This element of the strategy should provide every opportunity for children with low vision or who are blind to participate fully in the lesson. Advice to teachers is also that they should capitalise upon the 'strong visual element' of mathematics at every opportunity to 'illuminate meaning' (National Numeracy Strategy p. 21, cited in Arnold 2000).

The message we received from teachers and others during the inquiry was that children with VI could be successfully included in the National Numeracy Strategy, but that for the child to be able to participate fully in the lesson there were implications for resourcing. For example:

- The high demand for tactile resources means that preparation takes time.
- Additional competencies in Braille are required (by the teaching assistant).
- Extra equipment is needed in the lesson.
- Many questions need careful adaptation.
- Handouts require a simplified layout. Furthermore, even though the child might benefit from an easier-to-understand page format, he will require full exposure to all types of formats and diagrams in order to have the opportunity to succeed in SAT tests.

The extra workload required to meet the demands of the National Numeracy Strategy has resulted in some schools providing pre- or post-lesson tutoring. The importance of teachers planning lessons with teaching assistants well in advance – or at least of providing detailed lesson plans a week beforehand – was stressed many times.

> *With the Numeracy Hour . . . it isn't what they were doing, it was the speed. And because so much of the maths is visual, so, the mental maths, where the teacher was giving them various sums . . . our youngsters who were switched on were fine, the ones who were having problems with numbers or relationships would really be struggling and so we often had to take them out from the start.*
>
> [service member]

(For a helpful account of how to include children with severe VI in the National Numeracy Strategy, see Arnold 2000.)

Staff development session for non-specialists: Developing know-how

This session is intended for use by teachers and teaching assistants and is designed to be used independently, although some staff may wish to work on the tasks together and this is encouraged.

Reinforcing the additional curriculum

Identify ways in which you could help the child with VI to reinforce skills normally taught by the specialist teacher.

Mobility

Tactile awareness

Teaching and learning in the main classroom

It would be helpful if you were to identify a lesson which you have planned in concept already, but for which you have yet to prepare handouts or OHPs.

- What is the title of your chosen lesson?

- What is the aim of the lesson?

- What are the objectives?

- What materials will you need in order to deliver the lesson?

Task

Write a brief plan of the main activities intended to take place.

Activity	Time	Related objectives

Delivering the lesson

Below is a list of ways of enabling children with VI to participate more fully in the lesson.

- Make presentations as clear and easy to read as possible.
- Deliver the lesson through sound and touch as well as sight. For example, provide verbal description.
- Use real objects for a lesson.
- Utilise good listening skills.
- Refer to children by name.
- Give children time to formulate responses and complete tasks.
- Encourage group work.

Consider each of the suggestions in turn in relation to each of the activities that you have planned for the lesson. Perhaps these will include whole-class teaching, one-to-one work or small group work. You will need to decide which statements relate to each activity.

> Make presentations as clear and easy to read as possible.

Deliver the lesson through sound as well as sight. For example, provide verbal description.

Practise describing or explaining part of the lesson without any use of the visual media. This is more difficult than at first it might appear, as so often we rely on sight as a means of conveying information.

Try taping yourself and then play it back. Does it make sense? Follow your instructions exactly – are they detailed enough?

Use real objects for a lesson.

Gather together as many real objects as you can that are related to your selected lesson. This can be of benefit to all children, but in particular will enable a child with VI to learn through touch.

Ask a staff member, teaching assistant or teacher to spend a few minutes during the lesson observing you teach. Do you refer to children by name? Do you give all children the time they need to formulate responses and complete tasks?

Encouraging group work – is an element of group work planned for the lesson?

If the child with VI for whom you have responsibility uses Braille or Moon then spend a little time learning the basics of these modes of communication.

As an absolute minimum learn the name of the child in Braille or in Moon.

How else could you make the lesson more accessible to the child with visual impairment?

[Child's name] written in Braille or in Moon. Draw the pattern that the indentations make.

---

9 Towards the development of better practice

Introduction

So far, the focus of this book has been on the inclusion of the individual child with visual impairment. A child-centred approach to the development of inclusive practices has been adopted with attention concentrated on the learning and teaching of the child with VI; those people most closely associated with his/her education; and on the development of classroom practices. This approach facilitates understanding of the specific needs of the child and the development of practices supportive of that child. While it is argued that this is an entirely appropriate framework in which teachers and teaching assistants can learn together to develop collaborative working practices (pragmatically, because these are the people who need to work together on a daily basis), it is also suggested that the development of such practices may be best encouraged within the context of the whole school.

The real improvements taking place in schools are due to the determined efforts and work of teachers, head teachers and many others. Much can be gained from staff critically reflecting on their work and then sharing good ideas. This helps to identify areas for improvement (in research terms sometimes called a *performance gap*), which in turn can lead to changes in school policies and the establishment of better systems. Educational research should provide valuable and useful guidance to schools and feed into national and local policy on education. However, there is also much that can be achieved by teachers and others conducting investigations in school (*action research*). The staff development sessions in this book encourage teachers and others to reflect critically on their work, which is the first step towards embarking on action research. Once a performance gap is identified, more information may be required in order to make informed and appropriate changes grounded in the context of the school.

It is intended that the staff development sessions should help to develop closer collaboration between teachers and support assistants, draw attention to the needs of the child with VI, thereby stimulating the development of better practice for that child and others, and act as a stimulus to encourage critical reflection on practice for the purpose of making positive change.

The value of research in pedagogy

Although a whole-school approach to the development of a more inclusive school culture (and I would also argue that this *is* also synonymous with the development of an educationally more effective culture of learning and teaching) is of course necessary, much of the research in the field has taken as inherent an assumption that the development of managerial strategies and systems will have a positive impact on the quality of the teaching and learning in classrooms. No doubt, this managerialist assumption carries with it some truth; common sense tells us that a better organised school with whole-school systems designed to support those at risk of marginalisation is preferable to a school whose systems are less responsive to need or in which information is difficult to access. However, effective organisational practices cannot be assumed to reach to the essence of good teaching; surely, the quality of teaching and effective learning depends on the quality of interaction taking place between teacher and children. As Stubbs (1976: 99) has pointed out, 'a person cannot simply walk into a room and be a teacher: he or she has to do quite specific communicative acts . . . social roles such as "teacher" or "pupil" do not exist in the abstract. They have to be acted out, performed and continuously constructed in the course of social interaction.' Thus, in this book I have emphasised ways of increasing the participation of the child in the main activities taking place in the classroom and focused on developing the quality of interaction between the class teacher, child and support assistant.

In considering the nature of the teaching and learning taking place in the classroom, a number of assumptions have been made: that active learning methods will encourage social interaction and shared learning; that active learning methods such as genuine group work (in addition to the case of pupils working on common tasks individually and being allowed to talk to each other) are more responsive to a group of pupils with diverse needs; and that the process of learning is shaped by the children as well as the teacher. The transmission model of learning whereby pupils are viewed as passive recipients of knowledge passed on by the teacher should be rejected in favour of an approach that encourages creative thought and real engagement in the subject matter, and arguably in the long term the fruition of independent thinking and learning. Recognition of the social aspect of learning explains our discontent with LSAs working on a one-to-one basis with a child for *extensive* periods of time throughout the school day.

The other salient characteristic of our view of learning and teaching is the rejection of a separate pedagogy for children with special educational needs and disabilities. Pedagogy is needed that is suitable for all the children in the classroom. Although children with special educational needs might, for example, need to be taught at a slower pace and with more repetition, basically the methods of teaching should be the same as for the other children in the classroom; if the teacher is to take responsibility for the learning of the whole class, and if children with special or additional needs are to belong to that class, then they along with the other children need to share a commonality of experience. Such a pedagogy needs to utilise methods that enable children with limited sensory stimuli to participate in the process of learning, as multi-sensory approaches to teaching and learning tend to do. Experience shows that children with special educational needs, who by definition are likely to find learning more difficult, have most need for effective high quality teaching. These are also the children who lose out the most when classroom management is lacking, lessons are dull or learner engagement is not an inherent part of the teaching process. This is not to say that periods of withdrawal should not take place. On the contrary, withdrawal and one-to-one tuition can be very effective when in class, and the expectation is that for the vast majority of schools a unifed pedagogical approach is needed that is capable of responding to the diversity of children's needs in the class.

Focusing on the classroom, therefore, enables us to provide guidance on pedagogy and to address questions about the nature of teaching and learning, especially regarding how teachers can manage the learning of all children for whom they have responsibility. Failure to provide a specific focus on pedagogy by the community of special and inclusive education researchers has led to a lack of pedagogical development that has an inclusive perspective. This must be of some concern, for surely, if we are to philosophise, argue and work in various ways for the inclusion of children with special educational needs in mainstream schools, then as a field we should also be able to provide guidance for teachers in mainstream schools as to how best to manage and support the children that we consider are better provided for by the mainstream sector.

In order to understand why *more* pedagogical research with an inclusive perspective is needed it is helpful to recognise the significance of social difference. Many schools nowadays have a greater proportion of children with special educational needs and disabilities than was the case when much of the research on pedagogy was conducted; however, not only might more diversity be expected now in school, much of the existing research was conducted in middle-class 'white' areas, i.e. in schools whose contexts and circumstances are very different from those of many schools in other neighbourhoods (e.g. inner urban, ethnic minority, working class). Disregard of social difference in the design of research studies has resulted in the failure of those studies to recognise the environmental impact on the identity of children as learners, or the collective agency shaping classroom processes (e.g. Thrupp 1998), of a class of children whose socialisation is qualitatively different from the patterns of socialisation most valued and desired by teachers and by schools.

Moreover, I also argue that the dominance of normative assumptions, methods and means of analysis of research in pedagogy has tended to result in the bypassing of those children on the margins – i.e. those children who could be described as extreme cases – because this was not its purpose. For instance, as Plewis (1980) points out, the 'fifteen thousand hours study' (Rutter *et al.* 1979) excluded all but the middle band of children for important elements of analysis, and failed to discuss the fact that this restricts generalisation of their findings to only that middle band of children. In essence, there has been a largely unsung, but nevertheless deep-rooted assumption in the field of school effectiveness research that what works for the majority will also be of benefit for the minority, which in the main has gone unchallenged.

The thinking in the field of inclusive education is quite the opposite; our assumption is that what works for those on the margins will also benefit the majority. However, this also remains an assumption that needs testing if we really are to do justice to *all* children in the classroom. Certainly from a human rights perspective, we argue for the non-segregated socialisation of children with disabilities. We can also argue convincingly that by placing children with disabilities in mainstream schools, we are providing a mechanism for reducing prejudice and fear of difference in those children we regard as non-disabled or without special educational needs. However, surely, it should also be incumbent upon us to find out how methods of interaction and teaching that seem to work for those on the margins, really do impact on others, e.g. our most able children.

Reflections on the methodology

Multiple case study research – such as the research on the inclusion of children with VI in mainstream primary schools on which this book is based – seems to provide a way forward for pedagogical research. Schools or classrooms can be studied as interesting cases in their own right, but conducting multiple case studies also allows for the possibility of making analytical generalisations that could be of use to others as they strive to make their schools better places for children. The research findings seem to confirm the advantage of comparison and analysis of the context of teaching and learning in a substantial number of schools.

For instance, the research was able to contribute to knowledge about how to teach the child within the context of a mainstream classroom because it was based on careful consideration of 23 children with VI, all learning in different educational contexts. Focusing on one classification of need improved our understanding of that group of children, and also ensured that the specific needs of that group were not overlooked. The case studies provided examples of inclusion for the child in particular schools, but we were also able to identify emergent themes (the result of analytic generalisation) by systematically comparing the case studies. One important justification for taking a multiple case study approach is an 'adaptive' view of educational change. This approach values the special characteristics of local contexts and individual school cultures. While most of those working in the field of inclusive education take this view, there is still debate in the wider educational research community.

Although we do not yet know, as Hopkins *et al.* (1999) acknowledge, the extent of the 'context specificity' of the findings of research in schools against the 'universality' or 'generality' of the findings, it is clear that, at least in some circumstances, what is 'good' organisation and practice for some children may be less appropriate for others. For example, in the USA, Borich (1996) identified distinctly different, but overlapping sets of factors regarding the effective teaching of literacy for schools in areas of low socio-economic status and schools in areas of middle and high socio-economic status. All this points to the need for developing a better or more effective pedagogy that reflects the diversity of neighbourhoods, social difference, children's aspirations and the varied contexts and circumstances in which the schools operate. Multiple case study methodology accords with an adaptive view of change (as local contexts and individual schools' cultures are valued in the research design).

Apart from the knowledge gained about the inclusion of children with VI discussed earlier, it is evident that some of our findings – such as the collaboration of staff, tensions in the role of the support assistant or increasing the participation in lessons – apply to the teaching and learning of other children, both those regarded as having special educational needs and those that do not. (These themes are returned to in the staff development session at the end of this chapter.) We also conclude that many of the suggestions for making the curriculum more accessible to the child with VI are also of benefit to other children (e.g. multi-sensory approach, the need for careful planning of the lesson to allow sufficient time for the preparation of resources, clear and easy to read handouts etc.). Alternatively, there are instances when a teacher mindful of including a child with VI may not choose to work spontaneously, and a certain creativity on the part of the teacher may be relinquished.

Finally, teacher engagement in educational research deserves to be a valued part of the research process. For research to inform teaching it must be grounded in existing practices and have regard for the circumstances of schools. Otherwise, the findings will bypass the practitioners the research is intended to support (Robinson 1998). School staff will only consider making concerted efforts to bring about improvement when they perceive that there is first a need, and secondly a constructive and achievable means by which to bring about change. The educational research community has a key role in providing guidance to schools and policy makers. However, there is much to be gained from schools embarking on their own research for development. While this was not the nature of the VI research described herein, the staff development materials are intended to stimulate reflective thinking and perhaps act as a starting point for future research and development work.

As Hopkins (1994: 23) writes: 'we struggle to relate strategies and research knowledge to the realities of schools in a pragmatic, systematic and sensitive way'. I leave it to you as the reader to judge the applicability of this book to the realities of your school and experience.

I close by again thanking all those who allowed us access to their teaching, who shared ideas, information and concerns, and provided useful feedback on the staff development sessions.

Development session: Moving forward towards educational inclusion

Whole-school development session

Suggested time one hour
Led by the class teacher and teaching assistant of the child with VI.
The class teacher and teaching assistant will need to meet prior to conducting this session.

Sharing knowledge

To be completed by the class teacher and teaching assistant prior to the session and then used as a basis for group discussion.

● What are the child's particular likes and dislikes?

● What ways of working/teaching approaches or methods seem to facilitate quality interaction between you and the child?

● What teaching approaches/methods facilitate the social development of the child?

● What have you done to facilitate opportunities for developing the child's independence in class and more generally in school?

● What have you learnt about how best to go about teaching the child?

● What tips can you pass on about how you collaborate? For example, how do you manage lesson planning and, perhaps, the advance preparation of resources?

Impacting on the quality of teaching and learning

Identify examples of good practice regarding the child with VI that are also of benefit to other children in the class.

Are there examples of good teaching practices that are specific to the child with VI?

- What teaching methods seem to encourage better social interaction? (Discuss particular cases that contributed to encouraging an interaction-rich environment.)

- Consider the value of focusing on one child whose circumstances are atypical.

Towards a culture of critical reflection

Working in small groups (class teachers with support assistants):
- Think of ways in which you could increase the child's participation in the learning process.

- Identify a lesson in which you will try out your suggestion.

- Are there particular children that you believe it would be helpful to focus on?

- How will you monitor the lesson?

  Observation

  Conversations with the children

  Other

Useful addresses

British Journal of Visual Impairment (BJVI)
www.nasen.org.uk/bjvi/home
The *British Journal of Visual Impairment* is for all professionals concerned with children and adults who have a visual impairment and is a national forum for all views on related subjects.

ClearVision
www.clearvisionproject.org/
ClearVision is a UK postal lending library of mainstream children's books with added Braille.

Department for Education and Skills (DfES)
www.dfes.gov.uk

Guide Dogs for the Blind Association
Burghfield Common
Reading, RG7 3YG
Tel: 0870 600 2323
www.guidedogs.org.uk

Lawson Large Print
www.largeprint.org/
e.g. Oxford Reading Tree
Very useful site run by a qualified teacher of the visually impaired.

LOOK
Federation of families with visually impaired children.
www.look-uk.org/

National Association for Special Educational Needs (NASEN)
www.nasen.org.uk
Provides teachers, parents and SENCOs with access to books, support materials and newsletters.

National Blind Children's Society
Bradbury House
Market Street
Highbridge
Somerset, TA9 3BW
Tel: 01278 764764
www.nbcs.org.uk
Information and support for parents of visually impaired children and young people.

National Library for the Blind
Far Cromwell Road
Bredbury
Stockport, SK6 2SG
Tel: 0161 355 2000
www.nlbuk.org/
A free library service for visually impaired readers who want books in accessible formats.

Office for Standards in Education (Ofsted)
Alexandra House
33 Kingsway
London, WC2B 6SE
www.ofsted.gov.uk
Inspection reports for mainstream and special schools are available.

Parents for Inclusion
Unit 2
70 South Lambeth Road
London, SW8 1R
www.parentsforinclusion.org

Royal National Institute for the Blind (RNIB)
105 Judd Street
London, WC1H 9NE
Tel: 020 7388 1266
Fax: 020 7388 2034
www.rnib.org.uk/info/
Fact sheets on many eye conditions and syndromes.

VisAbility
Editorial address: RNIB Education and Employment Division
7 Poplar Street
Fisher Gate
Nottingham, NG1 1GP
Tel: 0115 852 6736.
www.rnib.org.uk/education/vis.htm
VisAbility is the termly magazine for parents and professionals concerned with the education of visually impaired children and young people. The magazine focuses primarily on children and young people who attend their local mainstream school or college, and covers issues such as the statementing process, daily living skills, National Curriculum developments, mobility and inclusion.

Bibliography

Ainscow, M., Farrell, P., Tweddle, D. and Malki, G. (1999) 'The role of LEAs in developing inclusive policies and practices', *British Journal of Special Education* **26**(3), 136–40.

Arnold, A. (2000) 'National Numeracy Strategy', *VisAbility* Summer, 8–11.

Arter, C., Mason, H. L., McCall, S., McLinden, M. and Stone, J. (1999) *Children with Visual Impairment in Mainstream Settings*. London: David Fulton Publishers.

Balshaw, M. and Farrell, P. (2002) *Teaching Assistants*. London: David Fulton Publishers.

Booth, T. (1995) 'Concepts for all?', in Clark, C., Dyson, A. and Millward, A. (eds) *Towards Inclusive Schools*. London: David Fulton Publishers.

Borich, G. (1996) *Effective Teaching Methods*. New York: Macmillan Press.

Chapman, E. and Stone, J. M. (1998) *The Visually Handicapped Child in Your Classroom*. London: Cassell.

Clark, C., Dyson, A. and Millward, A. (eds) (1999) *Towards Inclusive Schools*. London: David Fulton Publishers.

Clunies-Ross, L. and Franklin, A. (1997) 'Where have all the children gone?', *British Journal of Visual Impairment* **15**, 48–52.

Dawkins, J. (1991) *Models of Mainstreaming for Visually Impaired Pupils*. London: RNIB/HMSO.

Denzin, N. K. and Lincoln, Y. S. (1998) *Strategies of Qualitative Inquiry*. London: Sage Publications.

Department for Education and Employment (DfEE) (2000) *Draft Special Educational Needs Code of Practice*. London: DfEE.

Department for Education and Skills (DfES) (2001) *Special Educational Needs Code of Practice*. London: DfES.

Farrell, P., Balshaw, M. and Polat, F. (1999) *The Management, Role and Training of Learning Support Assistants*. DfEE Research Report No 161. Norwich: Crown.

Feiler, A. and Gibson, H. (1999) 'Threats to the inclusive movement'. *British Journal of Special Education* **26**(3), 147–52.

Greaney, J., Tobin, M. and Hill, E. (1999) *Braille Version of the Neale Analysis of Reading Abilities*. London: RNIB.

Hegarty, S., Lucas, D. and Pocklington, K. (1981) *Educating Pupils with Special Needs in the Ordinary School*. Windsor: NFER-Nelson.

Hopkins, D. (1994) 'Towards a theory for school improvement', in Gray, J. Reynolds, D. and Fitz-Gibbon, C. (eds) *Merging Traditions: The Future of Research on School Effectiveness and School Improvement*.

Hopkins, D., Gray, J. and Reynolds, D. (1999) 'Moving on and moving up: confronting the complexities of school improvement in the improving schools project'. *Educational Research and Evaluation* **5**(1), 22–40.

Lynas, W. (1999) 'Supporting the deaf child in the mainstream school: is there a best way?', *Support for Learning* **14**(3), 113–21.

McCall, S. (1999) in Arter *et al.* (1999).

Mason, H. L. and McCall, S. (eds) (1997) *Visual Impairment: Access to Education for Children and Young People.* London: David Fulton Publishers.

Mason, M. L. (1998) *Guidelines for Teachers and Parents of Young People with a Visual Impairment Using Low Vision Aids (LVAs).* Birmingham: University of Birmingham, School of Education.

Mittler, P. (1996) 'Preparing to teach all children', *Managing Schools Today* **6**(2), 13–15.

Mortimer, H. (1996) 'Welcoming young children with special needs into mainstream education', *Support for Learning* **10**(4), 164–9.

Plewis, I. (1980) 'Design and analysis: a comment', in B. Tizard (ed.) *Fifteen Thousand Hours: A Discussion.* London: University of London Institute of Education.

Quah, M. L. and Jones, K. (1997) 'Reshaping learning support in a rapidly developing society', *Support for Learning* **12**, 38–42.

Robinson, V. (1998) 'Methodology and the research-practice gap', *Educational Researcher* **27**(1), 17–26.

Rogers, S. and Roe, J. (1999) 'Pupils with vision impairment', in Berger and Gross (eds) *Teaching the Literacy Hour in an Inclusive Classroom.* London: David Fulton Publishers.

Rutter, M., Maughan, B., Mortimore, P. and Ouston, J. (1979) *Fifteen Thousand Hours: Secondary Schools and Their Effects on Children.* London: Open Books.

Sebba, J. and Sachdev, D. (1997) *What Works in Inclusive Education?* Barkingside: Barnardo's.

Stubbs, M. (1976) *Language, Schools and Classrooms.* London: Methuen.

Taylor, S. J. and Bogdan, R. (1984) *Introduction to Qualitative Research Methods: The Search for Meanings.* New York: Wiley.

Thrupp, M. (1998) 'Exploring the politics of blame: school inspection and its contestation in New Zealand and England, *Comparative Education* **34**(2), 195–209.

Torres, I. and Corn, A. L. (1990) *When You Have a Visually Handicapped Child in Your Classroom.* New York: American Foundation for the Blind.

Venables, K. (1998) 'Everyone belongs', *Special Children* (Jan.), 17–19.

Walker, E., Tobin, M. J. and McKennel, A. (1992) *Blind and Partially Sighted Children in Britain: The RNIB Survey*, Vol. 2. London: HMSO.

Webster, A. and Roe, J. (1998) *Children with Visual Impairments.* London: Routledge.

Welding, J. (1996) 'In-class support: a successful way of meeting individual need?', *Support for Learning* **11**(3), 113–17.

West, A. and Sammons, P. (1996) 'Children with and without "additional educational needs" at Key Stage 1 in six inner city schools – teaching and learning processes and policy implications', *British Educational Research Journal* **22**, 113–27.

Index